TRADITIONAL LACE KNITTING

TRADITIONAL LACE KNITTING

Furze Hewitt

Photography by Robert Roach
Line illustrations by Josephine Hoggan

Kangaroo Press

Dedicated to my grandchildren and their parents

Acknowledgments

This book would not have been possible without the expertise of the following people:

- Robert Roach, photographer, for his skill in photographing white cotton knitting.
- Josephine Hoggan, artist, for her delightful drawings.
- Dina Tagliapietra, for her typing skills.
- The knitters: Edna Lomas, Joan Eckersley, Ruth Rintoule, Barbara Hosking, Betty Featherstone, Dulcie Brewer, Thea Moore, Kathy Grin.
- Joan Jackson: master embroiderer.
- John Cummins of Queanbeyan Books and Prints, for his constant search for lace knitting patterns.
- Amanda Crutchley, and DMC Needlecraft Pty Ltd, for their continued interest in our work, and for supplying the DMC yarns used in producing the articles for the book.
- My appreciation to the following for their assistance: Roslyn Panetta, Isabel Bunting, Anne Savage, Michael Roath, Maurine Rogers, Keith Hewitt, Patsy Ranger, Gillian Colquhoun, Carol Davey, Patricia Wain, Patricia Walsh, Simon Cottee, Jane Cottee, Maree Lever, Pauline Kirk, Paddy Lloyd, Ria Warke, Jo Waring, Alexis McLachlan and Margaret Hutchings.

Technical note:
All the photographs in this book were taken using:

- Kodak Ektachrome Plus, Professional, 35 mm Daylight Slide Film, processed by Kodak.
- Zeiss Ikon/Voigtlander Icarex 35S camera with Carl Zeiss Ultron 50mm fl.8 lens (bought in 1970).

Front cover: Laurel Wreath Cloth (page 14), and Willow Basket Lid (page 99) in garden picnic setting
Frontispiece: Abbey Square (page 54)

© Furze Hewitt 1997

First published in 1997 by Kangaroo Press Pty Ltd
An imprint of Simon & Schuster Australia
20 Barcoo Street (PO Box 507)
East Roseville NSW 2069 Australia
Printed in Hong Kong through Colorcraft Ltd

ISBN 0 86417 859 X

Contents

'The Knitting Lesson': a charming reverse painting on glass from the author's collection

Introduction

The patterns in this book are from my collection of nineteenth century knitting publications. All these patterns have been deciphered and rewritten in present day terminology, thus preserving them for the future.

The designs have been worked by dedicated knitters, anxious to preserve this gentle craft of lace knitting.

Joan Jackson has enhanced several of the items with her exquisite embroidery, adding a touch of colour to the designs.

The delicate drawings are by Josephine Hoggan of Bright, Victoria. Jo's sensitive touch is apparent in her work.

Robert Roach is a master of his craft of photography. White lace knitting is not the easiest of subjects to photograph.

Some of the patterns are used in different applications to illustrate the versatility of the design, encouraging you to vary the use of yarn, and needles, to create a variety of textures, e.g. pattern 3, Calico Lace, is seen again on page 38 as pattern 13, Amy Rose, and in pattern 34, the Nandina Collection, as the cake circle. The small drink cover in pattern 12, page 36, is also seen as the preserve cover 'Tomato' in pattern 27 on page 70. All the patterns in this book can be used in this fashion, helping you to create your own individual style.

All of the items are worked in cotton. Cotton is inexpensive, readily available and durable.

Needles in smaller sizes are available to help you create fine laces. See Suppliers, page 103.

All of the patterns in this book are suitable for knitters of moderate skills.

Happy knitting.

Furze Hewitt, 1997

7

Abbreviations and Terms

Abbreviations are used in knitting instructions to save space, and to make the pattern easier to follow. It is important to read, and understand, the abbreviations before beginning to knit a pattern. In this book most of the patterns use standard British abbreviations.

In ordinary knitting the made sts consist of the following:

yfwd	between two knit stitches
yon	between a purl and knit action
yrn	between two purl actions

In this book the above actions are referred to as m1 (meaning make one, or more as indicated, e.g. m2, m3, etc.) as they are commonly written in old lace patterns.

yfwd	yarn forward
yon	yarn over needle
yrn	yarn around needle
RH	right hand
LH	left hand
tw st	twist stitch
inc	increase
dc	double crochet
ch	chain

Some helpful abbreviations

k	knit
p	purl
st	stitch
sts	stitches
b	back
f	front
sl	slip
wyib	with yarn in back
wyif	with yarn in front
tog	together
*m1	make 1 stitch by winding yarn around needle
turn	work is turned before end of row
dpn	double pointed needle
motif	design unit
st, st	stocking stitch—knit right side, purl wrong side
garter st	knit all rows
mb	make bobble
beg	beginning
psso	pass slipped stitch over
p2sso	pass 2 slipped stitches over
p-wise	purlwise
k-wise	knitwise
tbl	through back of loop
ybk	yarn back

Comparative terms

British	American
cast off	bind off
tension	gauge
alternate rows	every other row
miss	skip
work straight	work even
stocking stitch	stockinette stitch
shape cap	shape top

Knitting needle sizes

Metric	British	American
2 mm	14	00
2.25	13	0
2.75	12	1
3	11	2
3.25	10	3
3.75	9	4
4	8	5
4.5	7	6
5	6	7
5.5	5	8
6	4	9
6.5	3	10
7	2	$10^{1}/_{2}$
7.5	1	11
8	0	12
9	00	13
10	000	15

*In old knitting publications the increase in lace knitting was referred to in several different ways: o – over; m1 – make 1; and cast up.

Techniques

Casting on

Step 1

Step 2

Step 3

Step 4

Thumb method of casting on

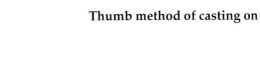

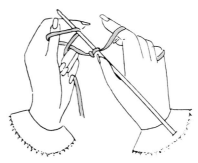

Step 1

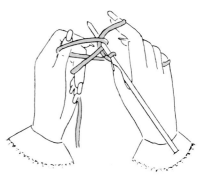

Step 2

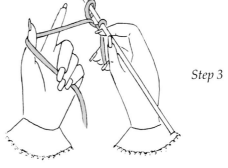

Step 3

How to knit

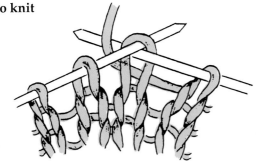

How to purl

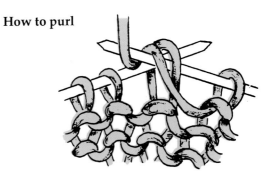

Invisible cast-on method

1. Using contrasting thread, cast on the number of stitches required, work two rows in stocking stitch
2. With main thread, continue work until length required.
3. When work is completed, remove contrasting thread. Either graft or sew together open stitches from both ends of work.

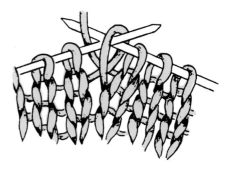

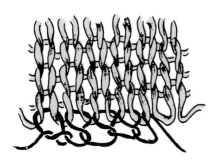

Invisible casting-on

Increasing in lace knitting

There are three methods of increasing the number of stitches in a row, or in a round. One way is to knit twice into a stitch (Fig. 1). This increase can be worked k-wise or p-wise. Read your pattern carefully and work as directed.

A second method is to pick up a loop between two sts, and knit into that loop (Fig. 2). This prevents a hole forming in the knitting.

The third method (Fig. 3), make one (or m1), produces the holes in lace knitting. The way it is worked depends on whether the extra stitch is to be made between two knit stitches, a knit and a purl, or two purl stitches. Between knit sts the yarn is brought forward, and over the needle as you knit the next stitch, thus forming a new stitch. Once again, read your pattern carefully.

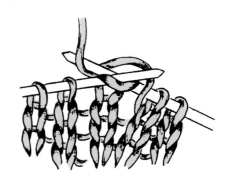

Fig. 2

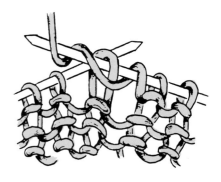

Fig. 3 (a) Make one between two knit stitches

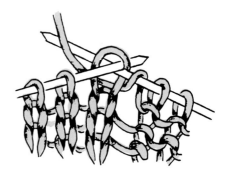

Fig. 3 (b) Make one between two purl stitches

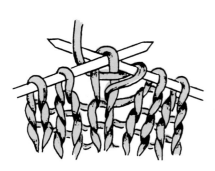

Fig. 1

Fig. 3 (c) Make one between a knit and a purl stitch

Decreasing in lace knitting

Again there are several methods. One method is to knit or purl two stitches together (Fig. 4a and b). A second method is to pass the second last stitch previously worked over the last one (Fig. 4c and d).

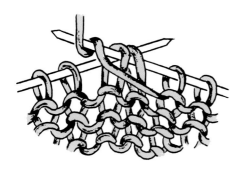

Fig. 4 (a)

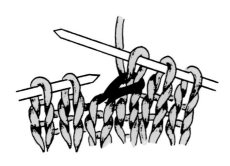

Fig. 4 (b)

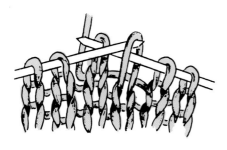

Fig. 4 (c)

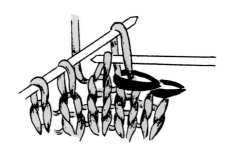

Fig. 4 (d)

Knitted picot cast-off

Knit 1st st. *Sl st from RH needle onto LH needle. Insert needle into this st, cast on 2 sts, then cast off 5 sts. Repeat from * until all sts have been cast off.

Knitting off your stitches if you can't crochet

K1, *k2 tog, m1, k2 tog, turn. P1, [(k1, p1) twice, k1] in next stitch.
P1, sl 1 p-wise, turn. Cast off 7 sts (1 st left on RH needle)*.
Repeat from * – * to last 5 sts. K3 tog, m1, k2 tog, turn, p1, (k1, p1) twice, k1, in next st, p1, sl 1 p-wise, turn. Cast off remaining sts.
For a larger loop on your edging, make 9 sts instead of the 5 sts just described.

Grafting

A simplified method from Barbara Hosking

Place two needles, each with an equal number of sts, wrong sides together.
   Thread bodkin with matching yarn. Insert bodkin k-wise into first st on front needle, slip off. Insert bodkin into second st p-wise, leave on needle. Insert bodkin through first st on back needle p-wise, slip off. Thread through second st k-wise, leave on needle. Repeat thus until grafting is completed.

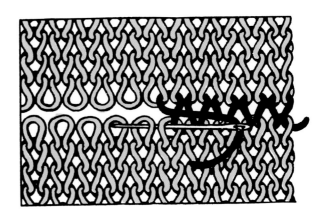

Grafting

Tension

Experienced knitters know if their tension varies from the average. Early knitting instructions rarely have given tensions. The chart below is a basic guide to assist knitters of average tension.

Basic tension table gives average tension in st, st over 25 mm (1")

Needle size	2-ply	3-ply	4-ply
12	9 sts	8½ sts	8 sts
11	8½ sts	8 sts	7½ sts
10	8 sts	7½ sts	7 sts
9	7½ sts	7 sts	6½ sts
8	7 sts	6½ sts	6 sts
7	6½ sts	6 sts	5½ sts

Lace knitters rely on their choice of yarn and needles and on the weight of the article being knitted, and adjust their knitting materials accordingly.

Suggested needles and cotton

Tray cloths, table cloths, small items of napery: Needles 2 mm (14), cotton 20
Lingerie: Needles 1. 75 mm (15), cottons 30–40
Infants' wear, lawn, linen, Liberty cottons: Needles 1.25 mm (18), cottons 80–100
Handkerchiefs, fine voiles and baptistes: Needles 1.00 mm (20), cottons 80–100

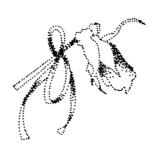

THE PATTERNS

1 LAUREL WREATH

A circular table topper featuring a wide leaf border. Knitted by Edna Lomas.

Materials

9 x 50 g balls 4-ply cotton
Needles 2.75 mm (12)
The cloth measures 132 cm (52") in diameter

Centre

Cast on 120 sts.
Row 1: knit
*Row ** 2:* k4. Turn
Row 3 and alternate rows: sl 1. Knit to end of row.
Row 4: k6, turn
Row 6: k8, turn
Row 8: k10, turn
Continue in this manner until you have worked k118, turn.
Next row: As row 3.
Next row: k4, *, m1, k2tog. Repeat from * to end of row.
Next row: knit **
Repeat **–** 11 times.
Cast off loosely.

Edging

Cast on 30 sts.
Row 1: k3, m1, k2tog, k1, p2, k1, k2tog, k6, p2, m1, k1, m1, p2, k3, m1, k2tog, k1, m2, k2.
Row 2: k3, p1, k3, m1, k2tog, k3, p3, k2, p5, p2tog, p1, k5, m1, k2tog, k1.

Row 3: k3, m1, k2tog, k1, p2, k1, k2tog, k4, p2, (k1, m1) twice, k1, p2, k3, m1, k2tog, k5.
Row 4: k7, m1, k2tog, k3, p5, k2, p3, p2tog, p1, k5, m1, k2tog, k1.
Row 5: k3, m1, k2tog, k1, p2, k1, k2tog, k2, p2, k2, m1, k1, m1, k2, p2, k3, m1, k2tog, k1, (m2, k2tog) twice.
Row 6: (k2, p1) twice, k3, m1, k2tog, k3, p7, k2, p1, p2tog, p1, k5, m1, k2tog, k1.
Row 7: k3, m1, k2tog, k1, p2, k1, k2tog, p2, k3, m1, k1, m1, k3, p2, k3, m1, k2tog, k7.
Row 8: k9, m1, k2tog, k3, p9, k2, p2tog, k5, m1, k2tog, k1.
Row 9: k3, m1, k2tog, k1, p2, m1, k1, m1, p2, k1, k2tog, k6, p2, k3, m1, k2tog, k1, (m2, k2tog) 3 times.
Row 10: (k2, p1) 3 times, k3, m1, k2tog, k3, p5, p2tog, p1, k2, p3, k5, m1, k2tog, k1.
Row 11: k3, m1, k2tog, k1, p2, (k1, m1) twice, k1, p2, k1, k2tog, k4, p2, k3, m1, k2tog, k10.
Row 12: k12, m1, k2tog, k3, p3, p2tog, p1, k2, p5, k5, m1, k2tog, k1.
Row 13: k3, m1, k2tog, k1, p2, k2, m1, k1, m1, k2, p2, k1, k2tog, k2, p2, k3, m1, k2tog, k2, (m2, k2tog) 4 times.
Row 14: (k2, p1) 4 times, k4, m1, k2tog, k3, p1, k2tog, p1, k2, p7, k5, m1, k2tog, k1.
Row 15: k3, m1, k2tog, k1, p2, k3, m1, k1, m1, k3, p2, k1, k2tog, p2, k3, m1, k2tog, k14.
Row 16: Cast off 11 sts. K4, m1, k2tog, k3, p2tog, k2, p9, k5, m1, k2tog, k1.
Repeat rows 1-16 until length desired.

2 ROISIN LACE

Lace edged continental pillow cases: A beautiful gift for a bride. Knitted by Betty Featherstone.

Materials
2 x 50 g balls DMC Cébélia
Needles 1.75 mm (15)
Large continental style pillowcases

Special abbreviations
1. Kpk: k1, p1, k1 into 1 stitch
2. Kpkp: k1, p1, k1, p1 into 1 stitch
The beading is a six-row pattern using four stitches:
Row 1: k4
Row 2: k4
Row 3: p2tog, m2, p2tog
Row 4: k2, p1, k1
Row 5: k4
Row 6: k4
Repeat rows 1-6. These will be referred to as edge 4.

Cast on 34 stitches. Knit one row loosely.
Commence pattern.
Row 1: m1, p2 tog, kpkp, m1, p2 tog, m1, k4 tog, kpk, k3 tog, kpk, m1, p2 tog, m1, k4 tog, kpk, k9, edge 4.
Row 2: Edge 4, k9, p22, m1, p2 tog
Row 3: m1, p2 tog, (kpk, k3 tog, kpk, m1, p2tog, m1, k4 tog) twice, kpk, k8, edge 4.
Row 4: Edge 4, k8, p25, m1, p2 tog.
Row 5: m1, p2 tog, (k3 tog, kpk) twice, m1, p2 tog, m1, k4 tog, kpk, k3 tog, kpk, m1, p2 tog, m1, k4 tog, kpk, k7, edge 4.
Row 6: Edge 4, k7, p26, m1, p2 tog.
Row 7: m1, p2 tog, (kpk, k3 tog) twice, kpk, m1, p2 tog, m1, k4 tog, kpk, k3 tog, kpk, m1, p2 tog, m1, k4 tog, kpk, k6, edge 4.
Row 8: Edge 4, k6, p29, m1, p2 tog.
Row 9: m1, p2 tog, (k3 tog, kpk) 3 times, m1, p2 tog, m1, k4 tog, kpk, k3 tog, kpk, m1, p2 tog, m1, k4 tog, kpk, k5, edge 4.

Row 10: Edge 4, k5, p30, m1, p2 tog.
Row 11: m1, p2 tog, (kpk, k3 tog) 3 times, kpk, m1, p2 tog, m1, k4 tog, kpk, k3 tog, kpk, m1, p2 tog, m1, k4 tog, kpk, k4, edge 4.
Row 12: Edge 4, k4, p33, m1, p2 tog.
Row 13: m1, p2 tog, (k3 tog, kpk) 4 times, m1, p2 tog, m1, k4 tog, kpk, k3 tog, kpk, m1, p2 tog, m1, k4 tog, kpk, k3, edge 4.
Row 14: Edge 4, k3, p34, m1, p2 tog.
Row 15: m1, p2 tog, (kpk, k3 tog) 3 times, (kpk, k4 tog, m1, p2 tog, m1, kpk, k3 tog) twice, k3, edge 4.
Row 16: Edge 4, k3, p35, m1, p2 tog.
Row 17: m1, p2 tog, (k3 tog, kpk) 3 times, k4 tog, m1, p2 tog, m1, kpk, k3 tog, kpk, k4 tog, m1, p2 tog, m1, kpk, k3 tog, k4, edge 4.
Row 18: Edge 4, k4, p30, m1, p2 tog.
Row 19: m1, p2 tog, (kpk, k3 tog), twice, (kpk, k4 tog, m1, p2 tog, m1, kpk, k3 tog) twice, k5, edge 4.
Row 20: Edge 4, k5, p29, m1, p2 tog.
Row 21: m1, p2 tog, (k3 tog, kpk) twice, k4 tog, m1, p2 tog, m1, kpk, k3 tog, kpk, k4 tog, m1, p2 tog, m1, kpk, k3 tog, k6, edge 4.
Row 22: Edge 4, k6, p27, m1, p2 tog.
Row 23: m1, p2 tog, kpk, k3 tog, (kpk, k4 tog, m1, p2 tog, m1, kpk, k3 tog) twice, k7, edge 4.
Row 24: Edge 4, k7, p25, m1, p2 tog.
Row 25: m1, p2 tog, k3 tog, kpk, k4 tog, m1, p2 tog, m1, kpk, k3 tog, kpk, k4 tog, m1, p2 tog, m1, kpk, k3 tog, k8, edge 4.
Row 26: Edge 4, k8, p22, m1, p2 tog.
Row 27: m1, p2 tog, k5 tog, m1, p2 tog, m1, kpk, k3 tog, kpk, k4 tog, m1, p2 tog, m1, kpk, k3 tog, k9, edge 4.
Row 28: Edge 4, k9, p18, m1, p2 tog.
Repeat rows 1-28 for length desired.

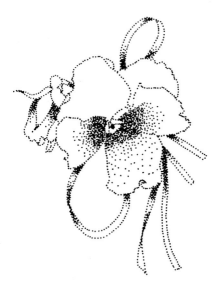

3 CALICO LACE

Ready-made calico curtains enhanced by lace knitting. Add a sash curtain for privacy or to obscure an uninteresting outlook. Lace by author.

Materials

20 x 50 g balls 4-ply cotton (approx.) for a pair of curtains
Needles 2 mm (14)
Sewing needle and cotton to sew lace to curtains

Cast on 33 sts.

Row 1: m1, k2 tog, sl 1, k2 tog, psso, (m2, sl 1, k2 tog, psso) 5 times, m2, k2 tog, k1, k2 tog, m2, k2 tog, k3, m1, k2 tog, k1.

Row 2: k8, p1, k4, p1, (k2, p1) 5 times, k2 tog, k1.

Row 3: m1, k2 tog, sl 1, k2 tog, psso, (m2, sl 1, k2 tog, psso) 4 times, m2, k2 tog, k3, k2 tog, m2, k2 tog, k2, m1, k2 tog, k1.

Row 4: k7, p1, k6, p1, (k2, p1) 4 times, k2 tog, k1.

Row 5: m1, k2 tog, sl 1, k2 tog, psso, (m2, sl 1, k2 tog, psso) 3 times, m2, k2 tog, k5, k2 tog, m2, k2 tog, k1, m1, k2 tog, k1.

Row 6: k6, p1, k8, p1, (k2, p1) 3 times, k2 tog, k1.

Row 7: m1, k2 tog, sl 1, k2 tog, psso, (m2, sl 1, k2 tog, psso) twice, m2, k2 tog, k7, k2 tog, m2, k2 tog, m1, k2 tog, k1.

Row 8: k5, p1, k10, p1, (k2, p1) twice, k2 tog, k1.

Row 9: m1, k2 tog, (sl 1, k2 tog, psso, m2) twice, k2 tog, k9, k2 tog, m1, k1, m1, k2 tog, k1.

Row 10: k17, p1, k2, p1, k3.

Row 11: m1, k2, (m2, sl 1, k2 tog, psso) twice, m2, k2 tog, k7, k2 tog, m2, k2 tog, m1, k2 tog, k1.

Row 12: k5, p1, k10, p1, (k2, p1) twice, k3.

Row 13: m1, k2, (m2, sl 1, k2 tog, psso) 3 times, m2, k2 tog, k5, k2 tog, m2, k2 tog, k1, m1, k2 tog, k1.

Row 14: k6, p1, k8, p1, (k2, p1) 3 times, k3.

Row 15: m1, k2, (m2, sl 1, k2 tog, psso) 4 times, m2, k2 tog, k3, k2 tog, m2, k2 tog, k2, m1, k2 tog, k1.

Row 16: k7, p1, k6, p1, (k2, p1) 4 times, k3.

Row 17: m1, k2, (m2, sl 1, k2 tog, psso) 5 times, m2, k2 tog, k1, k2 tog, m2, k2 tog, k3, m1, k2 tog, k1.

Row 18: k8, p1, k4, p1, (k2, p1) 5 times, k3.

Row 19: m1, k2, (m2, sl 1, k2 tog, psso) 7 times, m2, k2 tog, k4, m1, k2 tog, k1.

Row 20: k9, p1, (k2, p1) 7 times, k2 tog, k1.

Repeat rows 1–20 until length desired.

4 TOORA

Four lace-edged tea towels by Dulcie Brewer. Suitable for a gift. These towels have lace at each end for an attractive finish.

Materials
2 x 50 g balls DMC 20
Needles 2 mm (14)
Tea towels

TEA TOWEL 1

Cast on 4 sts.
Row 1: sl 1, k1, m2, k2.
Row 2: k3, p1, k2.
Row 3: sl 1, k5.
Row 4: k6.
Row 5: sl 1, k1, m2, k2 tog, m2, k2.
Row 6: k3, (p1, k2) twice.
Row 7: sl 1, k8.
Row 8: Cast off 5 sts, k3.
Repeat rows 1–8 until length desired.

TEA TOWEL 2

Cast on 6 sts.
Row 1: m1, p2 tog, k3. K in f & b of next st.
Row 2: k5, m1, p2 tog.
Row 3: m1, p2 tog, k1, (m2, k2 tog) twice.
Row 4: (k2, p1) twice, k1, m1, p2 tog.
Row 5: m1, p2 tog, k7.
Row 6: Cast off 3 sts. K3, m1, p2 tog.
Repeat rows 1-6 until length desired.

TEA TOWEL 3

Cast on 5 sts.
Row 1: k1, m1, k2 tog, m2, k2.
Row 2: k2, (k1, p1) in m2 of previous row, k3.
Row 3: k1, m1, k2 tog, k4.
Row 4: Cast off 2 sts. K4.
Repeat rows 1–4 until length desired.

TEA TOWEL 4

Cast on 7 sts.
Row 1: sl 1, p2, m1, p2 tog, m2, p2 tog.
Row 2: m1, k2, p1, k2, m1, k2 tog, k1.
Row 3: sl 1, p2, m1, p2 tog, p4.
Row 4: Cast off 2 sts. K3, m1, k2 tog, k1.
Repeat rows 1–4 until length desired.

5 GLADSTONE PARK LACE

A single bed sheet set with a beautiful nineteenth century lace edging.
Knitted by Barbara Hosking.

Materials
2 x 50 g balls DMC 20 Cébélia
Needles 2 mm (14)
Single bed sheet set

Cast on 34 sts.
Knit 3 rows.
Row 1: sl 1, (k4, m1, sl 1, k1, psso) twice, k3, k2 tog, m1, k1, m1, sl 1, k1, psso, k3, k2 tog, m1, sl 1, k1, psso, m1, k2, m1, k2 tog, k2.

Row 2: m1, k2 tog, k32.
Row 3: sl 1, k2 tog, m2, sl 1, k1, psso, k1, m1, sl 1, k1, psso, k4, m1, sl 1, k1, psso, k1, k2 tog, m1, k3, m1, sl 1, k1, psso, k1, k2 tog, m1, k2 tog, m1, k4, m1, k3.
Row 4: m1, k2 tog, k30, p1, k2.
Row 5: sl 1, k6, m1, sl 1, k1, psso, k4, m1, sl 1, k2 tog, psso, m1, k5, m1, sl 1, k2 tog, psso, m1, k2 tog, m1, k6, m1, k3.
Row 6: m1, k2 tog, k34.
Row 7: sl 1, k2, k2 tog, m2, sl 1, k1, psso, k1, m1, sl 1, k1,

22

psso, k4, m1, sl 1, k1, psso, k5, (k2 tog, m1) twice, k8, m1, k3.

Row 8: m1, k2 tog, k30, p1, k4.

Row 9: sl 1, k8, m1, sl 1, k1, psso, k4, m1, sl 1, k1, psso, k3, k2 tog, m1, k2 tog, m1, k10, m1, k3.

Row 10: m1, k2 tog, k36.

Row 11: sl 1, k2 tog, m2, sl 1, k1, psso, k2 tog, m2, sl 1, k1, psso, k1, m1, sl 1, k1, psso, k4, m1, sl 1, k1, psso, k1, k2 tog, m1, k2 tog, m1, k4, k2 tog, m2, sl 1, k1, psso, k4, m1, k3.

Row 12: m1, k2 tog, k8, p1, k21, p1, k3, p1, k2.

Row 13: sl 1, k10, m1, sl 1, k1, psso, k4, m1, sl 1, k2 tog, psso, m1, k2 tog, m1, k3, k2 tog, m2, sl 1, k1, psso, k2 tog, m2, sl 1, k1, psso, k3, m1, k3.

Row 14: m1, k2 tog, k7, p1, k3, p1, k26.

Row 15: sl 1, k2, k2 tog, m2, sl 1, k1, psso, k2 tog, m2, sl 1, k1, psso, k1, m1, sl 1, k1, psso, k4, m1, sl 1, k2 tog, psso, m1, k6, sl 1, k1, psso, m2, k2 tog, k6, m1, k3 (this is middle row of scallop).

Row 16: m1, k2 tog, k10, p1, k19, p1, k3, p1, k4.

Row 17: sl 1, k9, k2 tog, m1, k1, m1, sl 1, k1, psso, k4, (m1, sl 1, k1, psso) twice, k2, k2 tog, m2, sl 1, k1, psso, k2 tog, m2, sl 1, k1, psso, k2, k2 tog, m1, k2 tog, k2.

Row 18: m1, k2 tog, k7, p1, k3, p1, k26.

Row 19: sl 1, k2 tog, (m2, sl 1, k1, psso, k2 tog) twice, m1, k3, m1, sl 1, k1, psso, k4, (m1, sl 1, k1, psso) twice, k3, k2 tog, m2, sl 1, k1, psso, k3, k2 tog, m1, k2 tog, k2.

Row 20: m1, k2 tog, k8, p1, k21, p1, k3, p1, k2.

Row 21: sl 1, k7, k2 tog, m1, k5, m1, sl 1, k1, psso, k4, (m1, sl 1, k1, psso) twice, k8, k2 tog, m1, k2 tog, k2.

Row 22: m1, k2 tog, k36.

Row 23: sl 1, k2, k2 tog, m2, sl 1, k1, psso, k2 tog, m1, k7, m1, sl 1, k1, psso, k4, (m1, sl 1, k1, psso) twice, k6, k2 tog, m1, k2 tog, k2.

Row 24: m1, k2 tog, k30, p1, k4.

Row 25: sl 1, k5, k2 tog, m1, k1, m1, sl 1, k1, psso, k3, k2 tog, m1, k1, m1, sl 1, k1, psso, k4, (m1, sl 1, k1, psso) twice, k4, k2 tog, m1, k2 tog, k2.

Row 26: m1, k2 tog, k34.

Row 27: sl 1, k2 tog, m2, sl 1, k1, psso, k2 tog, m1, k3, m1, sl 1, k1, psso, k1, k2 tog, m1, k3, m1, sl 1, k1, psso, k4, (m1, sl 1, k1, psso) twice, k2, k2 tog, m1, k2 tog, k2.

Row 28: m1, k2 tog, k30, p1, k2.

Row 29: sl 1, k3, k2 tog, m1, k5, m1, sl 1, k2 tog, psso, m1, k5, m1, sl 1, k1, psso, k4 (m1, sl 1, k1, psso) twice, k2 tog, m1, k2 tog, k2.

Row 30: m1, k2 tog, k32 (34 sts).

Row 31: sl 1, k4, m1, sl 1, k1, psso, k3, k2 tog, m1, k1, m1, sl 1, k1, psso, k3, k2 tog, m1, sl 1, k1, psso, k4, m1, sl 1, k1, psso, m1, k2, m1, k2 tog, k2.

Row 32: m1, k2 tog, k32.

Row 33: sl 1, k2 tog, m2, sl 1, k1, psso, k1, m1, sl 1, k1, psso, k1, k2 tog, m1, k3, m1, sl 1, k1, psso, k1, k2 tog, m1, k4, (k2 tog, m1) twice, k4, m1, k3.

Row 34: m1, k2 tog, k30, p1, k2.

Row 35: sl 1, k6, m1, sl 1, k2 tog, psso, m1, k5, m1, sl 1, k2 tog, psso, m1, k4, k2 tog, m1, k2 tog, m1, k6, m1, k3.

Row 36: m1, k2 tog, k34.

Row 37: sl 1, k2, k2 tog, m2, sl 1, k1, psso, k1, m1, sl 1, k1, psso, k5, k2 tog, m1, k4, k2 tog, m1, k2 tog, m1, k8, m1, k3.

Row 38: m1, k2 tog, k31, p1, k4.

Row 39: sl 1, k8, m1, sl 1, k1, psso, k3, k2 tog, m1, k4, k2 tog, m1, k2 tog, m1, k10, m1, k3.

Row 40: m1, k2 tog, k36.

Row 41: sl 1, k2 tog, m2, sl 1, k1, psso, k2 tog, m2, sl 1, k1, psso, k1, m1, sl 1, k1, psso, k1, k2 tog, m1, k4, k2 tog, m1, k2 tog, m1, k4, k2 tog, m2, sl 1, k1, psso, k4, m1, k3

Row 42: m1, k2 tog, k8, p1, k21, p1, k3, p1, k2.

Row 43: sl 1, k10, m1, sl 1, k2 tog, psso, m1, k4, k2 tog, m1, k2 tog, m1, k3, k2 tog, m2, sl 1, k1, psso, k2 tog, m2, sl 1, k1, psso, k3, m1, k3.

Row 44: m1, k2 tog, k7, p1, k3, p1, k26.

Row 45: sl 1, k2, k2 tog, (m2, sl 1, k1, psso, k2 tog) twice, m1, k4, k2 tog, m1, k2 tog, m1, k6, k2 tog, m2, sl 1, k1, psso, k6, m1, k3 (this is middle row of a scallop).

Row 46: m1, k2 tog, k10, p1, k19, p1, k3, p1, k4.

Row 47: sl 1, k9, k2 tog, m1, k4, k2 tog, m1, k1, (m1, sl 1, k1, psso) twice, k2, k2 tog, m2, sl 1, k1, psso, k2 tog, m2, sl 1, k1, psso, k2, k2 tog, m1, k2 tog, k2.

Row 48: m1, k2 tog, k7, p1, k3, p1, k26.

Row 49: sl 1, k2 tog, (m2, sl 1, k1, psso, k2 tog) twice, m1, k4, k2 tog, m1, k3, (m1, sl 1, k1, psso) twice, k3, k2 tog, m2, sl 1, k1, psso, k3, k2 tog, m1, k2 tog, k2.

Row 50: m1, k2 tog, k8, p1, k21, p1, k3, p1, k2.

Row 51: sl 1, k7, k2 tog, m1, k4, k2 tog, m1, k5, (m1, sl 1, k1, psso), twice, k8, k2 tog, m1, k2 tog, k2.

Row 52: m1, k2 tog, k36.

Row 53: sl 1, k2, k2 tog, m2, sl 1, k1, psso, k2 tog, m1, k4, k2 tog, m1, k7, (m1, sl 1, k1, psso) twice, k6, k2 tog, m1, k2 tog, k2.

Row 54: m1, k2 tog, k30, p1, k4.

Row 55: sl 1, k5, k2 tog, m1, k4, k2 tog, m1, k1, m1, sl 1, k1, psso, k3, k2 tog, m1, k1, (m1, sl 1, k1, psso) twice, k4, k2 tog, m1, k2 tog, k2.

Row 56: m1, k2 tog, k34.

Row 57: sl 1, k2 tog, m2, sl 1, k1, psso, k2 tog, m1, k4, k2 tog, m1, k3, m1, sl 1, k1, psso, k1, k2 tog, m1, k3, (m1, sl 1, k1, psso) twice, k2, k2 tog, m1, k2 tog, k2.

Row 58: m1, k2 tog, k30, p1, k2.

Row 59: sl 1, k3, k2 tog, m1, k4, k2 tog, m1, k5, m1, sl 1, k2 tog, psso, m1, k5, (m1, sl 1, k1, psso) twice, k2 tog, m1, k2 tog, k2.

Row 60: m1, k2 tog, k32.

Repeat rows 1-60 until length desired.

6 RADIANT STAR

An attractive table centre or circular tray cloth. Knitted by Kathy Grin.

Materials
2 x 20 g balls DMC 20 cotton
Needles 2 mm (14)
60 cm circular needle
Crochet hook 0.75
Diameter of cloth 41 cm (16")

Cast on 8 sts: 2 sts on each of 2 needles, 4 sts on 3rd, work with 4th. Change to 60 cm circular needle on round 50. Use marker at beginning of each round. One section only of the pattern is given. Repeat 7 times, or to end of round.

Round 1: Knit.

Round 2: p1, m1.

Round 3: p1, k1, m1.

Round 4: p1, k2, m1.

Round 5: p1, k3, m1.

Round 6: p1, sl 1, k1, psso, m1, k2, m1.

Round 7: p1, k5, m1.

Round 8: p1, (sl 1, k1, psso, m1) twice, k2, m1.

Round 9: p1, k7, m1.

Round 10: p1, (sl 1, k1, psso, m1) 3 times, k2, m1.

Round 11: p1, k9, m1.

Round 12: p1, (sl 1, k1, psso, m1) 4 times, k2, m1.

Round 13: p1, k11, m1.

Round 14: p1, (sl 1, k1, psso, m1) 5 times, k2, m1.

Round 15: sl 1, k1, psso, k10, p1, m1, k1, m1.

Round 16: sl 1, k1, psso, (sl 1, k1, psso, m1) 4 times, k1, p1, k1, k twice in next st, k1.

Round 17: sl 1, k1, psso, k8, p1, m1, k4, m1.

Round 18: sl 1, k1, psso, (sl 1, k1, psso, m1) 3 times, k1, p1, k6.

Round 19: sl 1, k1, psso, k6, p1, m1, (k2, m1) 3 times.

Round 20: sl 1, k1, psso, (sl 1, k1, psso, m1) twice, k1, p1, k10.

Round 21: sl 1, k1, psso, k4, p1, m1, k3, m1, k4, m1, k3, m1.

Round 22: (sl 1, k1, psso) twice, m1, k1, p1, k14.

Round 23: sl 1, k1, psso, k2, p1, m1, k4, m1, k6, m1, k4, m1.

Round 24: sl 1, k1, psso, k1, p1, k18.

Round 25: sl 1, k1, psso, p1, m1, k5, m1, k3, m1, k2, m1, k3, m1, k5, m1.

Round 26: sl 1, k1, psso, k24.

Round 27: sl first st of each needle on to end of previous needle, k6, m1, (k4, m1) 3 times, k6, m1, k1, m1.

Round 28: Knit.

Round 29: k4, k2 tog, m1, k5, m1, (k2, m1) 3 times, k5, m1, sl 1, k1, psso, k4, m1, k3, m1.

Round 30: Knit.

Round 31: sl 1, k1, psso, k7, k2 tog, m1, k3, m1, k4, m1, k3, m1, sl 1, k1, psso, k7, k2 tog, m1, sl 1, k1, psso, m1, k1, m1, sl 1, k1, psso, m1.

Round 32: sl 1, k1, psso, k5, k2 tog, k14, sl 1, k1, psso, k5, k2 tog, k7.

Round 33: sl 1, k1, psso, k3, k2 tog, m1, k4, m1, k6, m1, k4, m1, sl 1, k1, psso, k3, k2 tog, m1, sl 1, k1, psso, m1, k3, m1, sl 1, k1, psso, m1.

Round 34: sl 1, k1, psso, k1, k2 tog, k18, sl 1, k1, psso, k1, k2 tog, k9.

Round 35: k3 tog, m1, k5, m1, k3, m1, k2, m1, k3, m1, k5, m1, k3 tog, m1, k2 tog, m1, k5, m1, sl 1, k1, psso, k1.

Round 36: Knit.

Round 37: sl first 2 sts of each needle onto end of previous needle.

Round 37: k3, k2 tog, m1, (k4, m1) 3 times, sl 1, k1, psso, k3, m1, (k2 tog, m1) twice, k1, k2 tog, m1, k1, m1, sl 1, k1, psso, k1, m1, (sl 1, k1, psso, m1) twice.

Round 38: Knit.

Round 39: sl 1, k1, psso, k5, k2 tog, m1, (k2, m1) 3 times, sl 1, k1, psso, k5, (k2 tog, m1) 3 times, k1, k2 tog, m1, k3, m1, sl 1, k1, psso, k1, m1, (sl 1, k1, psso, m1) twice.

Round 40: Knit.

Round 41: sl 1, k1, psso, k3, k2 tog, m1, k3, m1, k4, m1, k3, m1, sl 1, k1, psso, k3, k2 tog, m1, (k2 tog) twice, m1, k1, k2 tog, m1, k5, m1, sl 1, k1, psso, k1, m1, (sl 1, k1, psso) twice, m1.

Round 42: sl 1, k1, psso, k1, k2 tog, k14, sl 1, k1, psso, k1, k2 tog, k19.

Round 43: k3 tog, m1, k4, m1, (k3, m1) twice, k4, m1, k3 tog, m1, (k1, k2 tog, m1) 3 times, (k1, m1, sl 1, k1, psso) 3 times, k1, m1.

Round 44: Knit.

Round 45: sl first 2 sts on each needle onto end of previous needle (k2, k2 tog, m1) twice, k1, m1, (sl 1, k1, psso, k2, m1) twice, (k2 tog, m1, k1) 3 times, k2 tog, k3, (sl 1, k1, psso, k1, m1) 3 times, k2 tog, m1.

Round 46: Knit.

Round 47: sl 1, k1, psso, k3, k2 tog, m1, k3, m1, sl 1, k1, psso, k3, k2 tog, m1, (sl 1, k1, psso, k1, m1) 3 times, sl 1, k1, psso, k3 (k2 tog, m1, k1) 3 times, k2 tog, m1.

Round 48: sl 1, k1, psso, k1, k2 tog, k5, sl 1, k1, psso, k1, k2 tog, k25.

Round 49: k3 tog, m1, k5, m1, k3 tog, m1, (sl 1, k1, psso) twice, m1, (sl 1, k1, psso, k1, m1) twice, sl 1, k1, psso, (k1, k2 tog, m1) 3 times, (k2 tog) twice, m1.

Round 50 and alternate rows unless otherwise indicated: Knit.

Round 51: k9, m1, k1, m1, k9, m1, k3 tog, m1, k9, m1, k1, m1.

Round 53: k9, m1, k3, m1.

Round 55: k9, m1, k2 tog, m1, k1, m1, sl 1, k1, psso, m1.

Round 57: sl 1, k1, psso, k5, (k2 tog, m1) twice, k3, m1, sl 1, k1, psso, m1.

Round 59: sl 1, k1, psso, k3, (k2 tog, m1) 3 times, k1, m1, (sl 1, k1, psso, m1) twice.

Round 61: sl 1, k1, psso, k1, (k2 tog, m1) 3 times, k3, m1, (sl 1, k1, psso, m1) twice.

Round 63: sl 1, k2 tog, psso, m1, (k2 tog, m1) 3 times, k1, m1, (sl 1, k1, psso, m1) 3 times.

Round 65: k1, (k2 tog, m1) 3 times, k3, (m1, sl 1, k1, psso) 3 times.

Round 67: sl the last st of each RH needle on to the LH needle; sl 1, k2 tog, psso, m1, (k2 tog, m1) 3 times, k1, m1, (sl 1, k1, psso, m1) 3 times.

Round 68: Knit.

Repeat last 4 rows twice.

Round 77: k1, (k2 tog, m1) 3 times, k1, k twice into next st, k1, (m1, sl 1, k1, psso) 3 times.

Round 79: sl the last st of each RH needle onto LH needle; sl 1, k2 tog, psso, (k2 tog, m1) twice, (k3, m1) twice, sl 1, k1, psso, m1, sl 1, k1, psso.

Round 80: k8, k5 into next st, k7.

Round 81: sl the last st of RH needle onto LH needle; sl 1, k2 tog, psso, k2 tog, m1, k4, m1, k2 tog, m1, k1, m1, sl 1, k1, psso, m1, k4, m1, sl 1, k1, psso.

Round 83: sl the last st of each RH needle on to LH needle; sl 1, k2 tog, psso, k5, m1, k2 tog, m1, k3, m1, sl 1, k1, psso, m1, k5.

Round 85: k1, m1, sl 1, k1, psso, k1, (k2 tog, m1) twice, k5, (m1, sl 1, k1, psso) twice, k1, k2 tog, m1.

Round 87: k2, m1, sl 1, k2 tog, psso, m1, k2 tog, m1, sl 1, k1, psso, k3, k2 tog, m1, sl 1, k1, psso, m1, sl 1, k2 tog, psso, m1, k1.

Round 89: k1, k2 tog, m1, k1, m1, k2 tog, m1, k1, m1, sl 1, k1, psso, k1, k2 tog, (m1, k1, m1, sl 1, k1, psso) twice.

Round 90: Knit.

Round 91: sl last st of each RH needle on to LH needle. Insert hook in place near st just transferred. Pull thread through * (insert hook into next 3 sts as if to knit; thread over, pull thread through, thread over and pull through 2 loops; dc made; sl made sts from needle, 3 ch) twice. (Insert hook into next 2 sts; make dc as before, 7 ch) twice. Insert hook into next 3 sts and make dc as before. (7 ch, insert hook into next 2 sts and make dc as before) twice, 3 ch. Insert hook into next 3 sts and make dc as before, 3 ch. Repeat from * ending with sl st into 1st dc. Fasten off.

Dampen the work. Pin out to measurement, allow to dry.

26

7 WEB

An attractive cushion knitted by Ruth Rintoule. Joan Jackson made the cushion and embroidered the flowers.

Materials

1 x 50 g ball DMC Hermina
Set 4 dp needles 3 mm (11)
Circular needle 3 mm (11) 40 cm
DMC stranded embroidery threads for
    the floral design: Nos 221, 223, 224,
    225, 501, 502, 522
Calico cushion and insert.
Diameter of cushion: Approx 56 cm (22")

Cast on 312 sts.
Row 1: *, k2, p50. Repeat from * to end of round.
Row 2: As row 1.
Row 3: *, k2, p2 tog, p46, p2 tog. Repeat from * to end of round.
Row 4: *, k2, p48. Repeat from * to end of round.
Row 5: As row 4.
Row 6: *, k2, p2 tog, p44, p2 tog. Repeat from * to end of round.
Rows 7 and 8: Knit.
Row 9: *, k2, k2 tog, k42, sl 1, k1, psso. Repeat from * to end of round.
Rows 10 and 11: Knit.
Row 12: *, k2, k2 tog, k40, sl 1, k1, psso. Repeat from * to end of round. Work 6 purl rows, dec each side of the 2 knit sts. Knit 6 rows.
Continue decreasing until 36 sts remain, changing to dp needles when small enough.
Round 1: *, k2, k2 tog, sl 1, k1, psso. Repeat from * to end of round.
Round 2: Knit.
Round 3: (k2 tog) to end of round.
Round 4: (p2 tog) to end of round.
Break off cotton and thread through remaining sts. Fasten off.

8 AMARYLLIS

Dress designed and made by Joan Jackson for an antique Kley and Hahn doll c. 1902.
Lace trim by author. Doll's bonnet by author.

Materials

Dress:
3 x 20 g balls DMC 50 cotton
Needles 1.75 mm (16)

Bonnet:
1 x 50 g ball DMC Hermina 4-ply
Needles 2 mm (14)
Doll from author's collection measures 56 cm (22″)
The delightful bear escort, Pialligo, is from the Patricia Walsh collection.

Special instructions
k3 in next st = (k1, p1, k1) in m1 of previous row.
Cast off 3 sts = count the st left on needle.

DRESS

Cast on 24 sts.
NB: The 1st 4 rows are foundation rows.
Row 1: (k3, cast off 3 sts) 3 times, k6.
Row 2: k6, (m1, k3) 3 times.
Row 3: (k3, k3 in next st) 3 times, k6.
Row 4: Knit (24 sts).
*Row * 5:* Cast on 3 sts. Knit these 3 sts. (Cast off 3 sts, k3), 3 times, k6.
Row 6: k9, (m1, k3) 3 times.
Row 7: (k3, k3 in next st) 3 times, k9.
Row 8: Knit (27 sts).
Row 9: Cast on 3 sts (k3, cast off 3 sts) 3 times, k12.
Row 10: k12, (m1, k3) 3 times.
Row 11: (k3, k3 in next st) 3 times, k12.
Row 12: Knit (30 sts).
Row 13: Cast on 3 sts, (k3, cast off 3 sts) 3 times, k15.
Row 14: k15, (m1, k3) 3 times.
Row 15: (k3, k3 in next st) 3 times, k15.
Row 16: Knit (33 sts).
Row 17: (cast off 3 sts, k3) 3 times, cast off 3 sts, k12.
Row 18: k12, (m1, k3) 3 times.
Row 19: (k3, k3 in next st) 3 times, k12.
Row 20: Knit (30 sts).
Row 21: (Cast off 3 sts, k3) 3 times, cast off 3 sts, k9.
Row 22: k9, (m1, k3) 3 times.

Row 23: (k3. K3 in next st) 3 times, k9.
Row 24: Knit.
Row 25: (Cast off 3 sts, k3) 3 times, cast off 3 sts, k6.
Row 26: k6, (m1, k3) 3 times.
Row 27: (k3, k3 in next st) 3 times, k6.
Row 28: Knit (24 sts).
*Repeat rows 5–28 until length desired.

BONNET

Cast on 86 sts.
Work 4 rows k2, p2, rib.
Row 5: Knit.
Row 6: Purl.
Row 7: Knit.
Row 8: Purl.
Row 9: Knit.
Row 10: Purl.
Knit 4 rows.
Row 15: Purl.
Row 16: Knit.
Row 17: Purl.

NB: mb = make bobble (k3 in next st, turn, p3, turn, m1, k4, turn, p5, turn, k2 tog, k1, k2 tog, turn, p3, turn, sl 1, k2 tog, psso). Work thus when pattern reads mb.
Row 18: k5, *, mb, k4. Repeat from * to end of row.
Row 19: Purl.
Row 20: Knit.
Row 21: Purl.
Knit 3 rows
Repeat from row 15.
Row 35: Purl.
Row 36: Knit.
Repeat rows 35–36 three times.
Rows 43 and 44: Knit.
Row 45: p57, turn, leaving 29 sts on LH needle, k3, *, mb, k4. Repeat from * 5 times, k2 tog tbl, turn, p27, p2 tog, turn, k27, k2 tog, turn, p27, p2 tog.
Continue working on the bonnet crown in this manner. Make bobbles in every 6th row. Knitting between the purl rows. Dec 1 st at end of every row until 27 sts remain.
Cast off.

Frill for bonnet front

Cast on 86 sts.
Row 1: Knit.
Row 2: (m1, k1) to end of row.
Row 3: Knit.
Row 4: (m1, k1) to end of row.
Rows 5 and 6: Knit.
Cast off loosely.

Frill for back of bonnet

Cast on 86 sts.
Row 1: Knit.
Row 2: (m1, k1) to end of row.
Row 3: Knit.
Row 4: (m1, k1) to end of row.
Row 5: Knit.
Cast off loosely.
Sew front frilling by the cast-on sts to the row next to
the 1st 4 ribbed rows.

Sew frill for back of bonnet to the middle of the 9 knit
rows before commencement of crown. The frills will fall
into an even fullness if correctly attached.
Pick up and knit the sts across bottom of the bonnet at
neck edge
Knit 4 rows.
Make a row of holes thus:
K2, (m2, k2 tog, k2) to end of row.
Knit 4 rows.
Cast off.

Make two lengths of cord thus:
Cast on 3 sts using dp needle.
Row 1: * k3. Do not turn. Slide sts to other side of
needle.*
Repeat *–* until length desired.
Cast off.
Thread cords through holes, attaching the cords with
tiny sts inside the front of the bonnet. Adjust any fullness at the neck edge by drawing the cords together and
tying into a bow. A rosette could be placed at the front
cord ends if desired.

9 GINGHAM AND LACE

Pillows edged with knitted lace. Bottom pillow is trimmed with Beaconsfield Lace to match the antique blanket or coverlet protector (see pattern 10 on page 32). Top pillow is trimmed with a version of the popular Melon pattern.

Materials

DMC Cébélia 20 cotton
Needles 2 mm (14)
Approx 50 g cotton for a standard pillowcase.
Allow a generous amount of lace at each corner.

BEACONSFIELD LACE

Cast on 30 sts.

Row 1: sl 1, k2, m1, k2 tog, k1, k2 tog, m1, k1, (m1, k2 tog) twice, k7, (m1, k2 tog) 4 times, m1, k2.

Row 2: m1, k2 tog, k29.

Row 3: sl 1, k2, m1, (k2 tog) twice, m1, k3, (m1, k2 tog) twice, k7, (m1, k2 tog) 4 times, m1, k2.

Row 4: m1, k2 tog, k30.

Row 5: sl 1, k2, m1, k3 tog, m1, k2 tog, k1, k2 tog, (m1, k2 tog) twice, k7, (m1, k2 tog) 4 times, m1, k2.

Row 6: m1, k2 tog, k29.

Row 7: sl 1, k2, m1, k2 tog, k1, m1, k3, m1, k1, (m1, k2 tog) twice, k7, (m1, k2 tog) 4 times, m1, k2.

Row 8: m1, k2 tog, k32.

Row 9: sl 1, k2, m1, k2 tog, k2, m1, k3 tog, m1, k3, (m1, k2 tog) twice, k7, (m1, k2 tog) 4 times, m1, k2.

Row 10: m1, k2 tog, k33.

Row 11: sl 1, k2, m1, k2 tog, k6, k2 tog, m1, k2 tog, m1, k1, m1, k2 tog, k4, k2 tog, (m1, k2 tog) 5 times, k1.

Row 12: m1, k2 tog, k32.

Row 13: sl 1, k2, m1, k2 tog, k5, k2 tog, m1, k2 tog, m1, k3, m1, k2 tog, k2, k2 tog, (m1, k2 tog) 5 times, k1.

Row 14: m1, k2 tog, k31.

Row 15: sl 1, k2, m1, k2 tog, k4, k2 tog, (m1, k2 tog) twice, k1, k2 tog, m1, (k2 tog) twice, (m1, k2 tog) 5 times, k1.

Row 16: m1, k2 tog, k28.

Row 17: sl 1, k2, m1, k2 tog, k3, k2 tog, m1, k2 tog, m1, k1, m1, k3, m1, k1, k2 tog, (m1, k2 tog) 5 times, k1.

Row 18: m1, k2 tog, k29.

Row 19: sl 1, k2, m1, k2 tog, k2, k2 tog, m1, k2 tog, m1, k3, m1, k3 tog, m1, k1, k2 tog, (m1, k2 tog) 5 times, k1.

Row 20: m1, k2 tog, k28.

Repeat rows 1–20 until length desired.

BASIC MELON LACE

Cast on 25 sts.

Knit one row.

Row 1: sl 1, k3, p6, k3, m2, k2 tog, k to end of row.

Row 2: m1, k2 tog, k10, p1, k to end of row.

Row 3: sl 1, k3, p6, k to end of row.

Row 4: m1, k2 tog, k to end of row.

Row 5: sl 1, k3, p6, k3, (m2, k2 tog) twice, k to end of row.

Row 6: m1, k2 tog, k9, p1, k2, p1, k3, pass sts 4, 5, 6 over 1, 2, 3, m1, k1, m1, k2, m1, k4 (28 sts).

Row 7: sl 1, k3, p6, k to end of row.

Row 8: m1, k2 tog, k to end of row.

Row 9: sl 1, k3, p6, k3, (m2, k2 tog) 3 times, k to end of row.

Row 10: m1, k2 tog, k9, p1, (k2, p1) twice, k to end of row.

Row 11: sl 1, k3, p6, k to end of row.

Row 12: m1, k2 tog, k19, pass sts 4, 5, 6 over 1, 2, 3, m1, k1, m1, k2, m1, k4.

Row 13: sl 1, k3, p6, k3, (m2, k2 tog) 4 times, k to end of row (35 sts).

Row 14: m1, k2 tog, k10, (p1, k2) 3 times, p1, k to end of row.

Row 15: sl 1, k3, p6, k to end of row.

Row 16: m1, k2 tog, k to end of row.

Row 17: sl 1, k3, p6, k14, pass 8 sts over 2 sts, k3 tog.

Row 18: m1, k2 tog, k13, pass sts 4, 5, 6 over 1, 2, 3, m1, k1, m1, k2, m1, k4.

Repeat rows 1–18 until length desired.

10 SHELL OR FAN BEDSPREAD

A traditional shell or fan patterned bedspread with a fluted edging which follows the contours of the shell design around the four sides of the bedspread. Knitted by author.
Illustrated in the Gingham and Lace picture on page 31.

Materials
Approx 90 x 50 g balls 4-ply cotton
Needles 2 mm (14)

Measurements
Standard double bed size requires approximately 420 shells, plus 54 half shells. The half shells are used to even the sides of the bedspread. Knit sufficient fluted edging to trim all four sides.
These quantities are approximate only. The size will depend on the knitter's choice of bed size and materials.

Motif

Cast on 50 sts.
Row 1: Knit.
Row 2: k4, (k2 tog, m1) to last 4 sts, k4.
Row 3: Knit.
Row 4: k3, k2 tog. K to last 5 sts, k2 tog, k3.
Row 5: k4. P to last 4 sts, k4.
Row 6: As row 4.
Row 7: Knit.
Row 8: k4, (k2 tog, m1) to last 4 sts, k4.
Row 9: Knit.
Row 10: k3, k2 tog. K to last 5 sts, k2 tog, k3.
Row 11: k4, p to last 4 sts, k4.
Row 12: As row 10.
Row 13: As row 11.
Row 14: As row 5.
Row 15: As row 4.
Row 16: As row 5.

Row 17: As row 4.
Repeat last 8 rows until 8 sts remain. Knit, dec 1 st each end of alternate rows until 4 sts remain, sl 1, k3 tog, psso.
Cast off.

Half motifs for sides of bedspread

Cast on 26 sts.
Work as for full motif, making decreases on one edge only, keeping the other edge straight.
Cast off.

Fluted edging

Cast on 7 sts.
Row 1: Knit.
Row 2: k2, p5.
Row 3: k5, turn, p5.
Row 4: k6, turn, k1, p5.
Row 5: p5, k2.
Row 6: Knit.
Row 7: p5, turn, k5.
Row 8: p5, k1, turn, k6.
Repeat rows 1–8 until length desired.
Cast off.

Sew the fluted edging around the four sides of the bedspread. This enables you to turn the bedspread around, thus distributing the wear evenly.

11 HAMILTON SQUARE

Square table topper with tassels at each corner, knitted by Edna Lomas, placed over an attractive cloth. Also on the table are two knitted drink covers; the patterns for these appear on pages 36 and 37.

Materials
4 x 50 g balls DMC Hermina
Needles 2.75 mm (12)
Each motif 12.5 cm (approx. 5″)
Each square 25.5 cm (approx 10″)
Four tassels (1 x 50 g ball DMC Hermina will make 6 tassels)

Cast on 3 sts.
Row 1: Purl.
Row 2: (k1, m1) twice, k1.
Row 3: Purl.
Row 4: k1, (m1, k1) 4 times.
Row 5 and alternate rows: Purl.
Row 6: k1, m1, k2 tog, m1, k3, m1, k2 tog, m1, k1.
Row 8: k1, m1, k2 tog, m1, k5, m1, k2 tog, m1, k1.
Row 10: k1, m1, k2 tog, (m1, k1) twice, sl 1, k2 tog, psso, (k1, m1) twice, k2 tog, m1, k1.
Row 12: k1, m1, k2 tog, m1, k3, m1, sl 1, k2 tog, psso, m1, k3, m1, k2 tog, m1, k1.
Row 14: k1, m1, k2 tog, m1, k5, m1, k2 tog, k4, m1, k2 tog, m1, k1.
Row 16: k1, m1, k2 tog, [(m1, k1) twice, sl 1, k2 tog, psso, k1)] twice, m1, k1, m1, k2 tog, m1, k1.
Row 18: k1, m1, k2 tog, (m1, k3, m1, sl 1, k2 tog, psso) twice, m1, k3, m1, k2 tog, m1, k1.
Row 20: k1, m1, k2 tog, m1, k5, m1, k2 tog, k3, k2 tog, m1, k5, m1, k2 tog, m1, k1.
Row 22: k1, m1, k2 tog, [(m1, k1) twice, sl 1, k2 tog, psso, k1)] 3 times, m1, k1, m1, k2 tog, m1, k1.
Row 24: k1, m1, k2 tog, (m1, k3, m1, sl 1, k2 tog, psso) 3 times, m1, k3, m1, k2 tog, m1, k1.
Row 26: k1, m1, k2 tog, m1, k5, (m1, k2 tog, k4) 3 times, m1, k2 tog, m1, k1.
Row 28: k1, m1, k2 tog, m1, k25, m1, k2 tog, m1, k1.
Row 30: k1, m1, k2 tog, m1, k27, m1, k2 tog, m1, k1.
Row 32: k1, m1, k2 tog, m1, k29, m1, k2 tog, m1, k1.
Row 34: (k2 tog, m1) twice, k2 tog, k25, (k2 tog, m1) twice, k2 tog.
Row 36: (k2 tog, m1) twice, k2 tog, k23, (k2 tog, m1) twice, k2 tog.
Row 38: (k2 tog, m1) twice, k2 tog, k4, (m1, k2 tog, k4) twice, m1, k2 tog, k3, k2 tog, (m1, k2 tog) twice.
Row 40: k2 tog, m1, k2 tog, (m1, sl 1, k1, psso, k1, k2 tog, m1, k1) 3 times, m1, sl 1, k1, psso, k1, k2 tog, (m1, k2 tog) twice.

Row 42: (k2 tog, m1) twice, sl 1, k2 tog, psso, (m1, k3, m1, sl 1, k2 tog, psso) 3 times, (m1, k2 tog) twice.
Row 44: (k2 tog, m1) twice, k2 tog, k4, m1, sl 1, k1, psso, k3, k2 tog, m1, k4, k2 tog, (m1, k2 tog) twice.
Row 46: (k2 tog, m1) twice, [(k1, sl 1, k2 tog, psso, (k1, m1) twice)] twice, k1, sl 1, k2 tog, psso, k1, (m1, k2 tog) twice.
Row 48: (k2 tog, m1) twice, (sl 1, k2 tog, psso, m1, k3, m1) twice, sl 1, k2 tog, psso, (m1, k2 tog) twice.
Row 50: (k2 tog, m1) twice, k2 tog, k4, m1, k2 tog, k3, k2 tog, (m1, k2 tog) twice.
Row 52: (k2 tog, m1) twice, k1, sl 1, k2 tog, psso, (k1, m1) twice, k1, sl 1, k2 tog, psso, k1, (m1, k2 tog) twice.
Row 54: (k2 tog, m1) twice, sl 1, k2 tog, psso, m1, k3, m1, sl 1, k2 tog, psso, (m1, k2 tog) twice.
Row 56: (k2 tog, m1) twice, sl 1, k1, psso, k3, k2 tog, (m1, k2 tog) twice.
Row 58: (k2 tog, m1) twice, k1, sl 1, k2 tog, psso, k1, (m1, k2 tog) twice.
Row 60: (k2 tog, m1) twice, sl 1, k2 tog, psso, (m1, k2 tog) twice.
Row 62: k2 tog, m1, k2 tog, sl 1, k2 tog, psso, m1, k2 tog.
Row 63: p2, p2 tog, p2.
Row 64: k2 tog, k1, k2 tog.
Row 65: sl 1, p2 tog, psso.
Cast off.
Rows 1–65 form the motif. You need 4 motifs to form the pattern.

To make up
Press each square under a damp cloth. Join 4 motifs together to make the design. The blocks of 4 motifs are suitable for many projects: cot covers, bed covers, curtains and cushions. Shown here as a small table topper, the design could be extended to create a large tablecloth.

To fringe a cloth
Wind cotton thread around a 15 cm (6″) piece of card. Cut at one end making even lengths to form strands of fringe. Make a fringe of 5 strands in each open mesh of the design. Continue around the 4 sides of work.

The cloth could be finished with a knitted lace edging or, like the one shown, trimmed with simple tassels.

12 DRINK OR JUG COVERS

The beaded covers in the picture on page 34 date from the 1930s. These knitted covers, presently enjoying a great resurgence in popularity, are useful for protection against insects. The large cover was knitted by Ruth Rintoule, the small cover by the author.

Materials
Large cover: 1 x 20 g ball DMC 20 cotton
8 glass beads
Needles 1.25 mm (18)

Small cover: Portion of 1 x 20 g ball DMC 10 cotton
6 glass beads
Needles 2 mm (14)

Use antique hand-made beads if possible. These are often found attached to worn-out jug covers. The hand-made glass beads are worth recycling.

LARGE JUG COVER

Cast on 8 sts: 2 on 1st needle, 3 on each of 2 needles. Work with 4th needle.
Round 1: (m1, k1), repeat to end of round (16 sts).
Round 2: Knit.
Round 3: (m1, k1), repeat to end of round (32 sts).
Rounds 4, 5 and 6: Knit.
Round 7: (m1, k2 tog), repeat to end of round (32 sts).
Round 8: Knit.
Round 9: (m1, k1), repeat to end of round (64 sts).
Rounds 10 to 19: Knit.
Round 20: (m1, k8), repeat to end of round (72 sts).
Round 21 and all alternate rounds unless otherwise directed: Knit.
Round 22: (m1, k1, m1, k8), repeat to end of round (88 sts).
Round 24: (m1, k3, m1, sl 1, k1, psso, k4, k2 tog), repeat to end of round (88 sts).
Round 26: (m1, k5, m1, sl 1, k1, psso, k2, k2 tog), repeat to end of round.
Round 28: (m1, k7, m1, sl 1, k1, psso, k2 tog), repeat to end of round.
Round 30: (m1, k9, m1, k2 tog), repeat to end of round (96 sts).
Round 32: (m1, k11, m1, k1), repeat to end of round (112 sts).
Knit 7 rounds.

Continue thus:
Round 1: (m1, k13, m1, k1), repeat to end of round (128 sts).
Round 2 and every alternate round: Knit.
Round 3: k1, m1, (sl 1, k1, psso, k9, k2 tog, m1, k3, m1), repeat to end of round, ending each needle with m1, k2.
Round 4: To make pattern easier to follow take last 3 sts off needle and place on needle in front. Keep continuity of pattern as follows:
Round 5: (m1, k1, m1, k2 tog, m1, k2 tog, m1, sl 1, k1, psso, k7, k2 tog), repeat to end of round.
Round 7: (m1, k7, m1, sl 1, k1, psso, k5, k2 tog), repeat to end of round (128 sts).
Round 9: (m1, k1, m1, k2 tog, m1, k1, m1, k2 tog, m1, k2 tog, m1, k1, m1, sl 1, k1, psso, k3, k2 tog), repeat to end of round (144 sts).
Round 11: (m1, k13, m1, sl 1, k1, psso, k1, k2 tog), repeat to end of round.
Round 13: *(m1, k2 tog) 7 times, m1, k1, m1, sl 1, k2 tog, psso. Repeat from * to end of round (144 sts).
Round 15: (m1, k117, m1, k1), repeat to end of round.
Round 17: (m1, k2 tog), repeat to end of round,
Round 19: As round 17.
Round 21: (k9, inc 1 by knitting in f&b of next st), repeat to end of round (176 sts).
Round 23: (m1, k2 tog), repeat to end of round.
Round 25: (k10, inc 1 as in round 21), repeat to end of round.
Round 26: Knit to end of round (192 sts).
Commence point on 24 sts:
Row 1: (m1, k2 tog) 12 times, turn.
Row 2: p24, turn.
Row 3: k2 tog, k22, turn.
Row 4: p2 tog, p21, turn.
Row 5: k2 tog, *m1, k2 tog. Repeat from *, turn.
Row 6: p2 tog, p to end, turn.
Row 7: k2 tog, k to end, turn.
Row 8: As row 6. Turn.
Repeat rows 5–8 until 6 sts remain, then k2 tog 3 times, turn, k1, k2 tog, psso.
Cast off, leaving length of thread to attach bead at point. Work 7 more points.
Press the cover. Sew on beads.

SMALL DRINK COVER

Cast on 3 sts on each of 3 needles. Work with 4th needle.

Rounds 1 and 2: Knit.

Round 3: (m1, k1) to end of round.

Round 4 and alternate rounds: Knit.

Round 5: (m1, k2) to end of round.

Round 7: (m1, k3) to end of round.

Round 9: (m1, k4) to end of round.

Round 11: (m1, k5) to end of round.

Round 13: (m1, k6) to end of round.

Round 15: (m1, k1, m1, sl 1, k1, psso, k4) to end of round.

Round 17: (m1, k3, m1, sl 1, k1, psso, k3) to end of round.

Round 19: (m1, k2, m1, sl 1, k1, psso, k1, m1, sl 1, k1, psso, k2) to end of round.

Round 20: [(m1, k2, (m1, sl 1, k1, psso) twice, k1, m1, sl 1, k1, psso, k1)] to end of round.

Round 23: [(m1, k2, (m1, sl 1, k1, psso) 3 times, k1, m1, sl 1, k1, psso)] to end of round.

Round 25: [(m1, k2, (m1, sl 1, k1, psso) 5 times)] to end of round.

Round 26: knit (117 sts).

Purl 5 rows.

Cast off thus:

Knit 1st st, *sl 1 st from RH needle onto LH needle. Insert needle into this st. Cast on 2 sts, then cast off 5 sts. Repeat from * until all sts have been cast off.

13 AMY ROSE

A charming boudoir cushion, designed and made by Joan Jackson. Lace and braid knitted by author.

Materials

Make a basic cushion cover in the fabric of your choice. Joan has placed a diagonal square of fine linen, lined with pink cotton, in the centre of the cushion. The design of hemstitching and exquisite embroidery is outlined in knitted braid and lace edging.

DMC stranded embroidery thread was used for the floral design in the following shades: Nos 221, 223, 224, 225, 501, 502, 522.

Lace:

2 x 20 g balls DMC 20 cotton
Needles 1.25 mm (18)
Cushion measures 38 cm (15") square
Diagonal embroidered square 25.5 cm (approx. 10")
Lace 7.5 cm (3") wide
Knit the lace to edge the diagonal square, allowing ample fullness at the corners.

Braid:
Small quantity of DMC 100 cotton
Needle size 1 mm (20)

Lace

Cast on 33 sts.
Row 1: m1, k2 tog, sl 1, k2 tog, psso, (m2, sl 1, k2 tog, psso) 5 times, m2, k2 tog, k1, k2 tog, m2, k2 tog, k3, m1, k2 tog, k1.
Row 2: k8, p1, k4, p1, (k2, p1) 5 times, k2 tog, k1.
Row 3: m1, k2 tog, sl 1, k2 tog, psso, (m2, sl 1, k2 tog, psso) 4 times, m2, k2 tog, k3, k2 tog, m2, k2 tog, k2, m1, k2 tog, k1.
Row 4: k7, p1, k6, p1, (k2, p1) 4 times, k2 tog, k1.
Row 5: m1, k2 tog, sl 1, k2 tog, psso, (m2, sl 1, k2 tog, psso) 3 times, m2, k2 tog, k5, k2 tog, m2, k2 tog, k1, m1, k2 tog, k1.
Row 6: k6, p1, k8, p1, (k2, p1) 3 times, k2 tog, k1.
Row 7: m1, k2 tog, sl 1, k2 tog, psso, (m2, sl 1, k2 tog, psso) twice, m2, k2 tog, k7, k2 tog, m2, k2 tog, m1, k2 tog, k1.
Row 8: k5, p1, k10, p1, (k2, p1) twice, k2 tog, k1.
Row 9: m1, k2 tog, (sl 1, k2 tog, psso, m2) twice, k2 tog, k9, k2 tog, m1, k1, m1, k2 tog, k1.

Row 10: k17, p1, k2, p1, k3.
Row 11: m1, k2, (m2, sl 1, k2 tog, psso) twice, m2, k2 tog, k7, k2 tog, m2, k2 tog, m1, k2 tog, k1.
Row 12: k5, p1, k10, p1, (k2, p1) twice, k3.
Row 13: m1, k2, (m2, sl 1, k2 tog, psso) 3 times, m2, k2 tog, k5, k2 tog, m2, k2 tog, k1, m1, k2 tog, k1.
Row 14: k6, p1, k8, p1, (k2, p1) 3 times, k3.
Row 15: m1, k2, (m2, sl 1, k2 tog, psso) 4 times, m2, k2 tog, k3, k2 tog, m2, k2 tog, k2, m1, k2 tog, k1.
Row 16: k7, p1, k6, p1, (k2, p1) 4 times, k3.
Row 17: m1, k2, (m2, sl 1, k2 tog, psso) 5 times, m2, k2 tog, k1, k2 tog, m2, k2 tog, k3, m1, k2 tog, k1.
Row 18: k8, p1, k4, p1, (k2, p1) 5 times, k3.
Row 19: m1, k2, (m2, sl 1, k2 tog, psso) 7 times, m2, k2 tog, k4, m1, k2 tog, k1.
Row 20: k9, p1, (k2, p1) 7 times, k2 tog, k1.
Repeat rows 1–20 until length required.

Braid

Cast on 6 sts.
NB: This is a one-row pattern.
Sl 1, k2, m1, k2 tog, k1.
Work this row until length desired.
Knit four lengths for the cushion.

14 PANSIES

Four coathangers designed and knitted by Joan Eckersley.

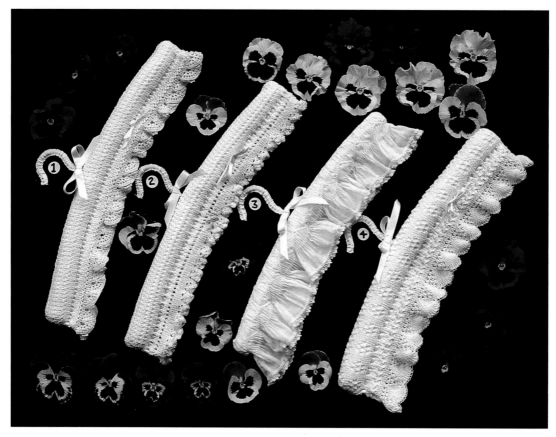

Materials
Plain coathangers
Wadding for padding
Ribbon for threading and bows

Coathanger 1:
2 x 20 g balls DMC Cébélia
Needles 2 mm (14)

Coathanger 2:
1 ball DMC Maeve
Needles 2mm (14)

Coathanger 3 (smocked coathanger edged with fine lace):
1 x 20 g ball DMC 100
Needles 1 mm (20)

Coathanger 4:
2 x 20 g balls DMC 10
Needles 2 mm (14)

COATHANGER 1

Make 2 pieces.
Cast on 26 sts.
Knit one row.
Row 1: sl 1, k1, m1, sl 1, k1, psso, k6, m1, sl 1, k1, psso, k8, m1, sl 1, k1, psso, k2, m3, k2 (29 sts).
Row 2: sl 1, k1, (k1, p1, k1) into m3 of previous row, k2, p2, k2, k2 tog, m2, k2 tog, k2, p2, k2, m1, k2 tog, k2, p2, k2 (29 sts).
Row 3: sl 1, k1, k2 tog, m1, k6, k2 tog, m1, k4, p1, k3, k2 tog, m1, k7 (29 sts).
Row 4: sl 1, k6, p2, k8, p2, k6, p2, k2 (29 sts).
Row 5: sl 1, k1, m1, sl 1, k1, psso, k6, m1, sl 1, k1, psso, k8, m1, sl 1, k1, psso, k2, (m1, k1) 5 times (34 sts).
Row 6: sl 1, k11, p2, k2, k2 tog, m2, k2 tog, k2, p2, k2, m1, k2 tog, k2, p2, k2 (34 sts).
Row 7: sl 1, k1, k2 tog, m1, k6, k2 tog, m1, k4, p1, k3, k2 tog, m1, k12 (34 sts).

Row 8: sl 1, k11, p2, k8, p2, k6, p2, k2 (34 sts).
Row 9: sl 1, k1, m1, sl 1, k1, psso, k6, m1, sl 1, k1, psso, k8, m1, sl 1, k1, psso, k2, (m1, k1) 10 times (44 sts).
Row 10: sl 1, k21, p2, k2, 2k2 tog, m2, k2 tog, k2, p2, k2, m1, k2 tog, k2, p2, k2 (44 sts).
Row 11: sl 1, k1, k2 tog, m1, k6, k2 tog, m1, k4, p1, k3, k2 tog, m1, k22 (44 sts).
Row 12: Cast off 18 sts. K3, p2, k8, p2, k6, p2, k2 (26 sts).
NB: Repeat from row 1, working row 11 thus:
After knitting last st, pick up and knit 8th st of previous scallop, counting from you, turn.
Work row 12, casting off 19 sts.

COATHANGER 2

Make 2 pieces.
Cast on 30 sts.
Row 1: Knit.
Row 2: sl 1, k7, (k2 tog, m2, k2 tog) twice, k2, (m1, sl 1, k1, psso) twice, k1, (m1, sl 1, k1, psso) twice, k3.
Row 3: sl 1, k15, p1, k3, p1, k9.
Row 4: sl 1, k29.
Row 5: As row 4.
Row 6: sl 1, k7, (k2 tog, m2, k2 tog) twice, k2, (m1, sl 1, k1, psso) twice, k1, (m1, sl 1, k1, psso) twice, k3.
Row 7: sl 1, k15, p1, k3, p1, k4, m2, (k1, m2) 3 times, k2 (38 sts).
Row 8: sl 1, (k2, p1) 4 times, k25.
Row 9: sl 1, k37.
Row 10: sl 1, k15, (k2 tog, m2, k2 tog) twice, k2, (m1, sl 1, k1, psso) twice, k1, (m1, sl 1, k1, psso) twice, k3.
Row 11: sl 1, k15, p1, k3, p1, k17.
Row 12: k12, wrapping yarn 3 times for each st, m3, k26.
Row 13: sl 1, k26, p1, k1; sl remaining 12 sts to RH needle, dropping extra loops and making 12 long loops. Sl the 12 loops back to LH needle. K tog as one st.
Repeat rows 2–13 until length desired, ending work on row 4.

COATHANGER 3

A pretty smocked coathanger edged with fine lace.

Edging
Cast on 8 sts.
Row 1: sl 1, k1, p2 tog, m1, k4 (8 sts).
Row 2: sl 1, k3, m1, k4 (9 sts).
Row 3: sl 1, k2, m1, p2 tog, m1, k4 (10 sts).
Row 4: sl 1, k3, m1, k2 tog, m1, k4, (11 sts).
Row 5: sl 1, k2, m1, (p2 tog, m1) twice, k4 (12 sts).
Row 6: Cast off 4 sts, k7 (8 sts).
Repeat rows 1–6 until length desired.

COATHANGER 4

Special abbreviation
3 over 3 = work thus: with yarn in knit position lift 1st 3 purled sts over last 3 sts, one at a time, on RH needle.

Make 2 pieces.
Cast on 46 sts.
Knit one row.
Row 1: sl 1, k2, p6, k9, k2 tog, m2, k2 tog, k2, p6, k3, m2, k13.
Row 2: m1, k2 tog, k12, p1, k13, p1, k19.
Row 3: sl 1, k2, p6, k3, k2 tog, m2, k2 tog, k8, p6, k18.
Row 4: m1, k2 tog, k32, p1, k13.
Row 5: sl 1, k2, p6, 3 over 3, k1, (k2 tog, m2, k2 tog) twice, k6, p6, 3 over 3, k3, m2, k2 tog, m2, k13 (51 sts).
Row 6: m1, k2 tog, k12, p1, k2, p1, k3, m1, k1, m1, k2, m1, k8, p1, k3, p1, k2, m1, k1, m1, k2, m1, k3.
Row 7: sl 1, k2, p6, k3, k2 tog, m2, k2 tog, k2, k2 tog, m2, k2 tog, k2, p6, k21.
Row 8: m1, k2 tog, k29, p1, k5, p1, k13.
Row 9: sl 1, k2, p6, k1, (k2 tog, m2, k2 tog) twice, k6, p6, k3, (m2, k2 tog) 3 times, k12 (54 sts).
Row 10: m1, k2 tog, k12, p1, (k2, p1) twice, k17, p1, k3, p1, k11.
Row 11: sl 1, k2, p6, 3 over 3, k3, k2 tog, m2, k2 tog, k8, p6, 3 over 3, k24.
Row 12: m1, k2 tog, k22, m1, k1, m1, k2, m1, k10, p1, k4, m1, k1, m1, k2, m1, k3.
Row 13: sl 1, k2, p6, k9, k2 tog, m2, k2 tog, k2, p6, k3, (m2, k2 tog) 4 times, k13 (58 sts)
Row 14: m1, k2 tog, k13, p1, (k2, p1) 3 times, k13, p1, k19.
Row 15: sl 1, k2, p6, k15, p6, k28.
Row 16: m1, k2 tog, k56.
Row 17: sl 1, k2, p6, 3 over 3, k15, p6, 3 over 3, k14, sl 1 onto RH needle. Lift 11 sts one by one over first st on LH needle. K the st, pass slipped st on RH needle over the st on LH needle, k1 (40 sts).
Row 18: m1, k2 tog, k14, m1, k1, m1, k2, m1, k15, m1, k1, m1, k2, m1, k3 (46 sts).
Repeat rows 1–18 until length desired.

To make up coathangers
Pad the wood. Insert hook in centre of hanger. Sew the 2 strips of knitting together, leaving a space in the centre for the hook. Place knitting over hanger. Thread ribbon through holes to link the cover together. Cover hook with ribbon or a knitted strip. Tie a ribbon bow at the base of the hook.

15 SEA SHELLS

Four charming hand towels with lace edgings beautifully knitted by Joan Eckersley.

Materials
Four hand towels
For each towel Joan used:
1 x 50 g ball DMC Cébélia 10
Needles 2 mm (14)

HAND TOWEL 1

Cast on 26 sts.
Knit one row.
Row 1: sl 1, k1, m1, k2 tog, k2, (m1, sl 1, k1, psso) twice, k1, k2 tog, m1, k3, m1, sl 1, k1, psso, k1, k2 tog, (m1, sl 1, k1, psso) k1.
Row 2: m1, k2 tog, k17, p4, k2.
Row 3: sl 1, k1, m1, k2 tog, k3, m1, sl 1, k1, psso, m1, sl 1, k2 tog, psso, m1, k5, m1, sl 1, k2 tog, psso, (m1, sl 1, k1, psso) twice, k1.
Row 4: m1, k2 tog, k15, p5, k2.
Row 5: sl 1, k1, m1, k2 tog, k4, m1, sl 1, k1, psso, m1, k1, m1, sl 1, k1, psso, k2 tog, m3, k2 tog, k1, m1, k1, (m1, sl 1, k1, psso) twice, k1.
Row 6: m1, k2 tog, k8, p1, k8, p6, k2.
Row 7: sl 1, k1, m1, k2 tog, k2, k2 tog, m1, sl 1, k1, psso, m1, k3, m1, sl 1, k1, psso, k3, k2 tog, m1, k3, m1, sl 1, k1, psso, m1, k2.
Row 8: m1, k2 tog, k19, p5, k2.
Row 9: sl 1, k1, m1, k2 tog, k1, k2 tog, m1, sl 1, k1, psso, m1, k5, m1, sl 1, k1, psso, k1, k2 tog, m1, k5, m1, sl 1, k1, psso, m1, k2.
Row 10: m1, k2 tog, k21, p4, k2.
Row 11: sl 1, k1, m1, (k2 tog) twice, (m1, sl 1, k1, psso) twice, k2 tog, m3, k2 tog, k1, m1, sl 1, k2 tog, psso, m1, sl 1, k1, psso, k2 tog, m3, k2 tog, k1, m1, sl 1, k1, psso, k2.
Row 12: m1, k2 tog, k6, p1, k9, p1, k6, p3, k2.
Row 13: sl 1, k1, m1, k2 tog, k2, (m1, sl 1, k1, psso) twice, k3, k2 tog, m1, k3, m1, sl 1, k1, psso, k3, k2 tog, (m1, sl 1, k1, psso) twice, k1.
Row 14: m1, k2 tog, k21, p4, k2.
Row 15: sl 1, k1, m1, k2 tog, k3, (m1, sl 1, k1, psso) twice, k1, k2 tog, m1, k5, m1, sl 1, k1, psso, k1, k2 tog, (m1, sl 1, k1, psso) twice, k1.
Row 16: m1, k2 tog, k19, p5, k2.
Row 17: sl 1, k1, m1, k2 tog, k4, m1, sl 1, k1, psso, m1, sl 1, k2 tog, psso, m1, sl 1, k1, psso, k3, k2 tog, m1, sl 1, k2 tog, psso, (m1, sl 1, k1, psso) twice, k1.
Row 18: m1, k2 tog, k15, p6, k2.
Row 19: sl 1, k1, m1, k2 tog, k2, k2 tog, m1, sl 1, k1, psso, m1, k3, m1, sl 1, k1, psso, k1, k2 tog, m1, k3, m1, sl 1, k1, psso, m1, k2.
Row 20: m1, k2 tog, k17, p5, k2.
Row 21: sl 1, k1, m1, k2 tog, k1, k2 tog, m1, sl 1, k1, psso, m1, k5, m1, sl 1, k2 tog, psso, m1, k5, m1, sl 1, k1, psso, m1, k2.
Row 22: m1, k2 tog, k19, p4, k2.
Row 23: sl 1, k1, m1, (k2 tog) twice, (m1, sl 1, k1, psso) twice, k2 tog, m3, k2 tog, (k1, m1) twice, sl 1, k1, psso, k2 tog, m3, k2 tog, k1, m1, sl 1, k1, psso, k2.
Row 24: m1, k2 tog, k6, p1, k9, p1, k6, p3, k2
Row 25: sl 1, k1, m1, k2 tog, k2, (m1, sl 1, k1, psso) twice, k3, k2 tog, m1, k3, m1, sl 1, k1, psso, k3, k2 tog, (m1, sl 1, k1, psso) twice, k1.
Row 26: m1, k2 tog, k21, p4, k2.
Row 27: sl 1, k1, m1, k2 tog, k3, (m1, sl 1, k1, psso) twice, k1, k2 tog, m1, k5, m1, sl 1, k1, psso, k1, k2 tog, (m1, sl 1, k1, psso) twice, k1.
Row 28: m1, k2 tog, k19, p5, k2.
Row 29: sl 1, k1, m1, k2 tog, k4, m1, sl 1, k1, psso, m1, sl 1, k2 tog, psso, m1, sl 1, k1, psso, k2 tog, m3, k2 tog, k1, m1, sl 1, k2 tog, psso, (m1, sl 1, k1, psso) twice, k1.
Row 30: m1, k2 tog, k8, p1, k8, p6, k2.
Row 31: sl 1, k1, m1, k2 tog, k2, k2 tog, m1, sl 1, k1, psso, m1, k3, m1, sl 1, k1, psso, k3, k2 tog, m1, k3, m1, sl 1, k1, psso, m1, k2.
Row 32: m1, k2 tog, k19, p5, k2.
Row 33: sl 1, k1, m1, k2 tog, k1, k2 tog, m1, sl 1, k1, psso, m1, k5, m1, sl 1, k1, psso, k1, k2 tog, m1, k5, m1, sl 1, k1, psso, m1, k2.
Row 34: m1, k2 tog, k21, p4, k2.
Row 35: sl 1, k1, m1, (k2 tog) twice, (m1, sl 1, k1, psso) twice, k3, k2 tog, m1, sl 1, k2 tog, psso, m1, sl 1, k1, psso, k3, k2 tog, m1, sl 1, k1, psso, m1, k2.
Row 36: m1, k2 tog, k19, p3, k2.
Repeat rows 1–36 until length required to fit the towel.

HAND TOWEL 2

Cast on 23 sts.
Knit one row.
Row 1: k3, m1, k2 tog, m1, sl 1, k2 tog, psso, m1, k2 tog, m1, k3, m1, k2 tog, m1, sl 1, k2 tog, psso, m1, k2 tog, m1, k3.
Row 2: m1, k20, m1, k2 tog, k1.
Row 3: k3, (m1, k2 tog) twice, (k2 tog, m1), twice, k1, (m1, k2 tog) twice, k1, k2 tog, m1, k5.
Row 4: m1, k21, m1, k2 tog, k1.
Row 5: k3, m1, k2 tog, m1, sl 1, k2 tog, psso, m1, k2 tog, m1, k3, m1, k2 tog, m1, sl 1, k2 tog, psso, m1, k7.
Row 6: m1, k22, m1, k2 tog, k1.
Row 7: k3, (m1, k2 tog) twice, k1, m1, k2 tog, m1, sl 1, k2 tog, psso, m1, k2 tog, m1, k3, m1, k8.
Row 8: m1, k24, m1, k2 tog, k1.
Row 9: k3, (m1, k2 tog) 4 times, k1, k2 tog, m1, k2 tog, m1, k1, m1, k2 tog, m1, k9.
Row 10: m1, k26, m1, k2 tog, k1.
Row 11: k3, (m1, k2 tog) twice, k1, m1, k2 tog, m1, sl 1,

k2 tog, psso, m1, k2 tog, m1, k3, m1, k2 tog, m1, k10.
Row 12: k9; pass 8 sts over 9th st; k19, m1, k2 tog, k1 (23 sts).
Repeat rows 1–12 until length required to fit towel.

HAND TOWEL 3

Special abbreviation
inc = k in f&b of st

Cast on 34 sts.
Row 1: sl 1, k2, m1, k2 tog, k2, (k2 tog, m1) 5 times, k9, (m1, k2 tog) twice, k2, inc, k1.
Row 2: k9, p9, k17.
Row 3: sl 1, k2, k2 tog, m1, k1, (k2 tog, m1) 6 times, k7, (m1, k2 tog) 3 times, k2, inc, k1.
Row 4: k11, p7, k18.
Row 5: sl 1, k2, m1, k2 tog, k2, (k2 tog, m1) 6 times, k5, (m1, k2 tog) 4 times, k2, inc, k1.
Row 6: k13, p5, k19.
Row 7: sl 1, k2, k2 tog, m1, k1, (k2 tog, m1) 7 times, k3, (m1, k2 tog) 5 times, k2, inc, k1.
Row 8: k15, p3, k20.
Row 9: sl 1, k2, m1, k2 tog, k2, (k2 tog, m1) 7 times, k1, (m1, k2 tog) 6 times, k2, inc, k1.
Row 10: k17, p1, k21.
Row 11: sl 1, k2, k2 tog, m1, k1, (k2 tog, m1) 5 times, k11, (m1, k2 tog) 4 times, k2, inc, k1.
Row 12: k13, p11, k16.
Row 13: sl 1, k2, m1, k2 tog, k2, (k2 tog, m1) 4 times, k13, (m1, k2 tog) 4 times, k2, inc, k1.
Row 14: k13, p13, k15.
Row 15: sl 1, k2, k2 tog, m1, k1, (k2 tog, m1) 4 times, k3, (k2 tog, m1) twice, k1, (m1, k2 tog) twice, k3, (m1, k2 tog) 4 times, k2, inc, k1.
Row 16: k13, p15, k14
Row 17: sl 1, k2, m1, k2 tog, k2, (k2 tog, m1) 3 times, k3, (k2 tog, m1) twice, k3, (m1, k2 tog) twice, k3, (m1, k2 tog) 4 times, k2, inc, k1.
Row 18: k13, p17, k13.
Row 19: sl 1, k2, k2 tog, m1, k1, (k2 tog, m1) 3 times, k3, (k2 tog, m1) twice, k1, m1, k3 tog, m1, k1, (m1, k2 tog) twice, k3, (m1, k2 tog) 4 times, k2, inc, k1.
Row 20: k1, k2 tog, k10, p19, k12.
Row 21: sl 1, k2, m1, k2 tog, k2, (k2 tog, m1) 3 times, k3, (k2 tog, m1) twice, k3, (m1, k2 tog) twice, k3, (m1, k2 tog) 4 times, k5.
Row 22: k1, k2 tog, k10, p17, k13.
Row 23: sl 1, k2, k2 tog, m1, k1, (k2 tog, m1) 4 times, k3, (k2 tog, m1) twice, k1, (m1, k2 tog) twice, k3, (m1, k2 tog) 4 times, k5.
Row 24: k1, k2 tog, k10, p15, k14.
Row 25: sl 1, k2, m1, k2 tog, k2, (k2 tog, m1) 4 times,

k13, (m1, k2 tog) 4 times, k5.
Row 26: k1, k2 tog, k10, p13, k15.
Row 27: sl 1, k2, k2 tog, m1, k1, (k2 tog, m1) 5 times, k11, (m1, k2 tog) 4 times, k5.
Row 28: k1, k2 tog, k10, p11, k16.
Row 29: sl 1, k2, m1, k2 tog, k2, (k2 tog, m1) 7 times, k1, (m1, k2 tog) 6 times, k5.
Row 30: k1, k2 tog, k14, p1, k21.
Row 31: sl 1, k2, k2 tog, m1, k1, (k2 tog, m1) 7 times, k3, (m1, k2 tog) 5 times, k5.
Row 32: k1, k2 tog, k12, p3, k20.
Row 33: sl 1, k2, m1, k2 tog, k2, (k2 tog, m1) 6 times, k5, (m1, k2 tog) 4 times, k5.
Row 34: k1, k2 tog, k10, p5, k19.
Row 35: sl 1, k2, k2 tog, m1, k1, (k2 tog, m1) 6 times, k7, (m1, k2 tog) 3 times, k5.
Row 36: k1, k2 tog, k8, p7, k18.
Row 37: sl 1, k2, m1, k2 tog, k2, (k2 tog, m1) 5 times, k9, (m1, k2 tog) twice, k5.
Row 38: k1, k2 tog, k6, p9, k17.
Row 39: sl 1, k2, k2 tog, m1, k1, (k2 tog, m1) 5 times, k11, (m1, k2 tog) twice, k3.
Row 40: k7, p11, k16.
Repeat rows 1–40 until length required to fit towel.

HAND TOWEL 4

Cast on 38 sts.
Knit one row.
Row 1: sl 1, k2, (m1, k2 tog) 3 times, k2, (k2 tog, m1) 3 times, k5, k2 tog, m2, k2 tog, k3, (k2 tog, m1) 3 times, k2 tog, k1.
Row 2: m1, k2 tog, k11, p1, k23.
Row 3: sl 1, k12, (m1, k2 tog) 3 times, k1, (k2 tog, m2, k2 tog) twice, k3, (m1, k2 tog) twice, m1, k2.
Row 4: m1, k2 tog, k10, p1, k3, p1, k21.
Row 5: sl 1, k2, (m1, k2 tog) 3 times, k5, (m1, k2 tog) 3 times, k2, k2 tog, m2, k2 tog, k6, (m1, k2 tog) twice, m1, k2.
Row 6: m1, k2 tog, k13, p1, k23.
Row 7: sl 1, k14, (m1, k2 tog) 3 times, k12, (m1, k2 tog) twice, m1, k2.
Row 8: m1, k2 tog, k38.
Row 9: sl 1, k2, (m1, k2 tog) 3 times, k7, (m1, k2 tog) 3 times, k5, k2 tog, m2, k2 tog, k3, (m1, k2 tog) twice, m1, k2.
Row 10: m1, k2 tog, k10, p1, k28.
Row 11: sl 1, k16, (m1, k2 tog) 3 times, k2, (k2 tog, m2, k2 tog) twice, k2, (m1, k2 tog) twice, m1, k2.
Row 12: m1, k2 tog, k9, p1, k3, p1, k26.
Row 13: sl 1, k2, (m1, k2 tog) 3 times, k9, (m1, k2 tog) 3 times, k3, k2 tog, m2, k2 tog, k5, (m1, k2 tog) twice, m1, k2.

44

Row 14: m1, k2 tog, k12, p1, k28.
Row 15: sl 1, k18, (m1, k2 tog) 3 times, (k2 tog, m2, k2 tog) twice, k4, (m1, k2 tog) twice, m1, k2.
Row 16: m1, k2 tog, k11, p1, k3, p1, k26.
Row 17: sl 1, k2, (m1, k2 tog) 3 times, k11, (m1, k2 tog) 3 times, k1, k2 tog, m2, k2 tog, k7, (m1, k2 tog) twice, m1, k2.
Row 18: m1, k2 tog, k14, p1, k28.
Row 19: sl 1, k20, (m1, k2 tog) 3 times, k12, (m1, k2 tog) twice, m1, k2.
Row 20: m1, k2 tog, k44.
Row 21: sl 1, k2, (m1, k2 tog) 3 times, k13, (m1, k2 tog) 3 times, k5, k2 tog, m2, k2 tog, k3, (m1, k2 tog) twice, m1, k2.
Row 22: m1, k2 tog, k10, p1, k34.
Row 23: sl 1, k22, (m1, k2 tog) 3 times, k2, (k2 tog, m2, k2 tog) twice, k2, (m1, k2 tog) twice, m1, k2.
Row 24: m1, k2 tog, k9, p1, k3, p1, k32.
Row 25: sl 1, k2, (m1, k2 tog) 3 times, k15, (m1, k2 tog) 3 times, k3, k2 tog, m2, k2 tog, k5, (m1, k2 tog) twice, m1, k2.
Row 26: m1, k2 tog, k12, p1, k34.
Row 27: sl 1, k21, (k2 tog, m1) 3 times, k3, (k2 tog, m2, k2 tog) twice, k1, (k2 tog, m1) 3 times k2 tog, k1.
Row 28: m1, k2 tog, k9, p1, k3, p1, k32.
Row 29: sl 1, k2, (m1, k2 tog) 3 times, k12, (k2 tog, m1) 3 times, k6, k2 tog, m2, k2 tog, k2, (k2 tog, m1) 3 times, k2 tog, k1.
Row 30: m1, k2 tog, k10, p1, k34.
Row 31: sl 1, k19, (k2 tog, m1) 3 times, k12, (k2 tog, m1) 3 times, k2 tog, k1.
Row 32: m1, k2 tog, k44.
Row 33: sl 1, k2, (m1, k2 tog) 3 times, k10, (k2 tog, m1) 3 times, k3, k2 tog, m2, k2 tog, k5, (k2 tog, m1) 3 times, k2 tog, k1.
Row 34: m1, k2 tog, k13, p1, k29.
Row 35: sl 1, 17, (k2 tog, m1) 3 times, k2, (k2 tog, m2, k2 tog) twice, k2, (k2 tog, m1) 3 times, k2 tog, k1.
Row 36: m1, k2 tog, k10, p1, k3, p1, k27.
Row 37: sl 1, k2, (m1, k2 tog) 3 times, k8, (k2 tog, m1) 3 times, k5, k2 tog, m2, k2 tog, k3, (k2 tog, m1) 3 times, k2 tog, k1.
Row 38: m1, k2 tog, k11, p1, k29.
Row 39: sl 1, k15, (k2 tog, m1) 3 times, k4, (k2 tog, m2, k2 tog) twice, (k2 tog, m1) 3 times, k2 tog, k1.
Row 40: m1, k2 tog, k8, p1, k3, p1, k27.
Row 41: sl 1, k2, (m1, k2 tog) 3 times, k6, (k2 tog, m1) 3 times, k7, k2 tog, m2, k2 tog, k1, (k2 tog, m1) 3 times, k2 tog, k1.
Row 42: m1, k2 tog, k9, p1, k29.
Row 43: sl 1, k13, (k2 tog, m1) 3 times, k12, (k2 tog, m1) 3 times, k2 tog, k1.
Row 44: m1, k2 tog, k38.
Row 45: sl 1, k2, (m1, k2 tog) 3 times, k4, (k2 tog, m1) 3 times, k3, k2 tog, m2, k2 tog, k5, (k2 tog, m1) 3 times, k2 tog, k1.
Row 46: m1, k2 tog, k13, p1, k23.
Row 47: sl 1, k11, (k2 tog, m1) 3 times, k2, (k2 tog, m2, k2 tog) twice, k2, (k2 tog, m1) 3 times, k2 tog, k1.
Row 48: m1, k2 tog, k10, p1, k3, p1, k21 (38 sts).
Repeat rows 1–48 until length required to fit towel.

To make up
Attach lace to towel with tiny sts. Add motif or ribbon bow to the towel and thread with ribbons if desired.

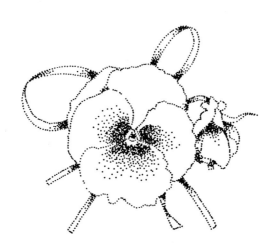

16 ENDYMION

Afternoon tea using an heirloom cloth. The lace pattern has been replicated by Ruth Rintoule and included here for your enjoyment.

Materials
White linen tablecloth of a size to meet your requirements.
Suggested thread, DMC 40 cotton, needles 1.25 mm (18).

Endymion can be worked in a coarser thread for heavier household items. Quantities of yarn are not given, as the amount required will depend on the size of the cloth and the knitter's preference.

Special abbreviations

mh = (sl 1, k1, psso, m2, k2 tog)

inc = k in f & b of st

Cast on 46 sts.

Knit one row.

Row 1: sl 1, k1, m1, sl 1, k1, psso, k5, p1, k25, p1, k10.

Row 2: k46.

Row 3: sl 1, k2, m1, sl 1, k1, psso, k6, mh, 4 times, k1, mh, k7, m1, k1, m3, k1, inc.

Row 4: k4, p1, k11, m3, (k3, p1) 4 times, k2, m3, k11.

Row 5: sl 1, k3, m1, sl 1, k1, psso, k6, p1, k20, p1, k8, (m1, k2 tog) twice, k5.

Row 6: Cast off 2 sts, k48.

Row 7: sl 1, k4, m1, sl 1, k1, psso, k6, mh, k4, sl 1, k1, psso, m2, k2 tog, k5, mh, k7, (m1, k2 tog) 3 times, m3, k1, inc.

Row 8: k4, p1, k15, m3, k7, p1, k6, m3, k13.

Row 9: sl 1, k5, m1, sl 1, k1, psso, k6, p1, k16, p1, k8, (m1, k2 tog) 4 times, k5.

Row 10: Cast off 2 sts, k50.

Row 11: sl 1, k6, m1, sl 1, k1, psso, k6, mh twice, k1, mh, k7, (m1, k2 tog) 5 times, m3, k1, inc.

Row 12: k4, p1, k19, m3, k3, p1, k3, p1, k2, m3, k15.

Row 13: sl 1, k7, m1, sl 1, k1, psso, k6, p1, k12, p1, k8, (m1, k2 tog) 6 times, k5.

Row 14: Cast off 2 sts, k52.

Row 15: sl 1, k8, m1, sl 1, k1, psso, k6, mh, k5, mh, k7, (m1, k2 tog) 7 times, m3, k1, inc.

Row 16: k4, p1, k23, m3, k6, m3, k17.

Row 17: sl 1, k9, m1, sl 1, k1, psso, k6, (p1, k8) twice, (m1, k2 tog) 8 times, k5.

Row 18: Cast off 2 sts, k54.

Row 19: sl 1, k10, m1, sl 1, k1, psso, k6, mh, k1, mh, k7, (m1, k2 tog) 9 times, m3, k1, inc.

Row 20: k4, p1, k27, m3, k2, m3, k19.

Row 21: sl 1, k11, m1, sl 1, k1, psso, k6, p1, k4, p1, k8, (m1, k2 tog) 10 times, k5.

Row 22: Cast off 2 sts, k56.

Row 23: sl 1, k1, (sl 1, k1, psso, m2, k2 tog) twice, k3, m1, sl 1, k1, psso, k6, mh, k8, (m1, k2 tog) 11 times, m3, k1, inc.

Row 24: k4, p1, k32, m3, k13, (p1, k3) twice.

Row 25: sl 1, k13, m1, sl 1, k1, psso, k6, p1, k9, (m1, k2 tog) 12 times, k5.

Row 26: Cast off 2 sts, k58.

Row 27: sl 1, k3, sl 1, k1, psso, m2, k2 tog, k7, m1, sl 1, k1, psso, k14, (m1, k2 tog) 13 times, m3, k1, inc.

Row 28: k4, p1, k52, p1, k5.

Row 29: sl 1, k12, k2 tog, m1, k16, k2 tog, (m1, k2 tog) 12 times, k6.

Row 30: Cast off 3 sts, k58.

Row 31: sl 1, k1, (sl 1, k1, psso, m2, k2 tog) twice, k2, k2 tog, m1, k7, mh, k7, k2 tog, (m1, k2 tog) 11 times, m3, k2 tog, inc.

Row 32: k4, p1, k32, m3, k13, (p1, k3) twice.

Row 33: sl 1, k10, k2 tog, m1, k9, p1, k10, k2 tog, (m1, k2 tog) 10 times, k6.

Row 34: Cast off 3 sts, k56.

Row 35: sl 1, k9, k2 tog, m1, k7, mh, k1, mh, k6, k2 tog, (m1, k2 tog) 9 times, m3, k2 tog, inc.

Row 36: k4, p1, k27, m3, k2, m3, k19.

Row 37: sl 1, k8, k2 tog, m1, k9, p1, k4, p1, k9, k2 tog, (m1, k2 tog) 8 times, k6.

Row 38: Cast off 3 sts, k54.

Row 39: sl 1, k7, k2 tog, m1, k7, mh, k5, mh, k6, k2 tog, (m1, k2 tog) 7 times, m3, k2 tog, inc.

Row 40: k4, p1, k23, m3, k6, m3, k17.

Row 41: sl 1, k6, k2 tog, m1, k9, p1, k8, p1, k9, k2 tog, (m1, k2 tog) 6 times, k6.

Row 42: Cast off 3 sts, k52.

Row 43: sl 1, k5, k2 tog, m1, k7, mh, (sl 1, k1, psso, m2, k2 tog) twice, k1, mh, k6, k2 tog, (m1, k2 tog) 5 times, m3, k2 tog, inc.

Row 44: k4, p1, k19, m3, k3, p1, k3, p1, k2, m3, k15.

Row 45: sl 1, k4, k2 tog, m1, k9, p1, k12, p1, k9, k2 tog, (m1, k2 tog) 4 times, k6.

Row 46: Cast off 3 sts, k50.

Row 47: sl 1, k3, k2 tog, m1, k7, mh, k4, sl 1, k1, psso, m2, k2 tog, k5, mh, k6, k2 tog, (m1, k2 tog) 3 times, m3, k2 tog, inc.

Row 48: k4, p1, k15, m3, k7, p1, k6, m3, k13.

Row 49: sl 1, k2, k2 tog, m1, k9, p1, k16, p1, k9, k2 tog, (m1, k2 tog) twice, k6.

Row 50: Cast off 3 sts, k48.

Row 51: sl 1, k1, k2 tog, m1, k7, m.h, (sl 1, k1, psso, m2, k2 tog) 4 times, k1, mh, k6, k2 tog, m1, k2 tog, m3, k2 tog, inc.

Row 52: k4, p1, k11, m3, (k3, p1) 4 times, k2, 0p1, k17.

Row 54: Cast off 3 sts, k46.

Row 55: sl 1, k7, m.h, k4, sl 1, k1, psso, m2, k2 tog, k4, sl 1, k1, psso, m2, k2 tog, k6, mh, k6, k2 tog, k1.

Row 56: k9, m3, k8, p1, k7, p1, k6, m3, k8.

Repeat rows 1–56 until length required to fit table cloth.

17 FEATHER AND FAN

An elegant table topper in the familiar feather and fan pattern. Edna Lomas of Hamilton knitted this useful cloth. The eight tassels complement the scalloped edge, and add a Victorian touch.

Materials
6 x 50 g balls 4-ply cotton
Needles 2.75 mm (12)
8 tassels
Sewing thread for attaching tassels

Make four.
Cast on 272 sts.
Rows 1 and 2: Knit.
Row 3: *(k2 tog) 3 times. (Pick up and k the thread that lies between the needles, k1) 5 times. Pick up 1, (k2 tog) 3 times. Repeat from * to end of row.
Row 4: **dec, k to last 2 sts, dec.
Row 5: As row 4.
Row 6: dec, p to last 2 sts, dec.
Row 7: k3 tog, k2, (pick up 1, k1) 3 times, *pick up 1, (k2 tog) 6 times, (pick up 1, k1) 5 times. Repeat from * until 20 sts remain. Pick up 1, (k2 tog) 6 times, (pick up 1, k1) 3 times, pick up 1, k2, k3 tog.
Rows 8 and 9: As row 4.
Row 10: As row 6.
Row 11: k2 tog, (pick up 1, k1) twice, *pick up 1, (k2 tog) 6 times, (pick up 1, k1) 5 times. Repeat from * until 16 sts remain. Pick up 1, (k2 tog) 6 times, (pick up 1, k1) twice, pick up 1, k2 tog.
Rows 12 and 13: As row 4.
Row 14: As row 6.
Row 15: k2, (k2 tog) 5 times, *(pick up 1, k1) 5 times, pick up 1, (k2 tog) 6 times. Repeat from * until 17 sts remain. (Pick up 1, k1) 5 times, pick up 1, (k2 tog) 5 times, k2.
Rows 16 and 17: As row 4.

Row 18: As row 6.
Row 19: k3 tog, (k2 tog) twice, *(pick up 1, k1) 5 times, pick up 1, (k2 tog) 6 times. Repeat from * until 12 sts remain. (Pick up 1, k1) 5 times, pick up 1, (k2 tog) twice, k3 tog**
Repeat **–** 6 times.
Rows 116 and 117: As row 6.
Row 118: As row 6.
Row 119: k3 tog, k2, (pick up 1, k1) 3 times, pick up 1, (k2 tog) 6 times, (pick up 1, k1) 3 times, pick up 1, k2, k3 tog.
Row 120 and 121: As row 4.
Row 122: As row 6.
Row 123: k2 tog, (pick up 1, k1) twice, pick up 1, (k2 tog) 6 times, (pick up 1, k1) twice, pick up 1, k2 tog.
Rows 124 and 125: As row 4.
Row 126: As row 6.
Row 127: k1, pick up 1, k1, (k2 tog) 4 times, k1, pick up 1, k1.
Rows 128 and 129: As row 4.
Row 130: dec, p2, dec.
Row 131: (k2 tog) twice.
Row 132: p2 tog.
Fasten off.

To make up
Sew the four sections together neatly, leaving sts rather loose to allow for stretching. Dampen the table cloth and pin out to a square. Allow to dry naturally. Attach tassels to each corner and centre of each side if desired.

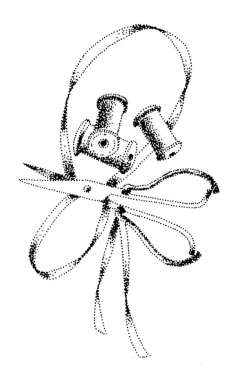

18 HEXAGON

An unusual doily in a hexagon shape. Made by Edna Lomas.

Materials
2 x 50 g balls DMC Hermina 4-ply
Needles 2.75 mm (12)

Measurement
38 cm (15") diameter

Cast on 6 sts; 2 sts on each of 3 needles, work with 4th needle.
Round 1: Knit.
Round 2: (m1, k1) to end of round.

Round 3 and alternate rounds: Knit.
Round 4: (m1, k2) to end of round.
Round 6: (m1, k1, k twice in next st, k1) to end of round.
Round 8: (m1, sl 1, k1, psso, k1, k2 tog) to end of round.
Round 10: (m1, k1, m1, sl 1, k2 tog, psso) to end of round.
Round 12: (m1, k3, m1, k1) to end of round.
Round 14: (m1, sl 1, k1, psso, k1, k2 tog, m1, k1) to end of round.
Round 16: k1, (m1, sl 1, k2 tog, psso, m1, k3). Repeat to last 2 sts, m1, k2.
Round 18: k2, (m1, k1, m1, k5). Repeat to end of round,

ending last repeat m1, k3.

Round 20: (m1, k2 tog, m1, k3, m1, k2 tog, m1, k1) to end of round.

Round 22: k1, m1, k1, (m1, sl 1, k1, psso, k1, k2 tog, m1, k1, m1, k3, m1, k1). Repeat to end of round, ending last repeat k1, k2 tog, m1, k1, m1, k2.

Round 24: k2, (m1, k2 tog, m1, sl 1, k2 tog, psso, m1, k2 tog, m1, k5). Repeat to end of round, ending last repeat m1, k2 tog, m1, k3.

Round 26: k3, (m1, sl 1, k1, psso, k1, k2 tog, m1, k7). Repeat to end of round, ending last repeat k4.

Round 28: (m1, k3, m1, sl 1, k1, psso, k1, k2 tog, m1, k3, m1, k1). Repeat to end of round.

Round 30: k1, (m1, k4, m1, sl 1, k2 tog, psso, m1, k4, m1, k3). Repeat to end of round, ending last repeat m1, k2.

Round 32: k2, (m1, k4, m1, k3, m1, k4, m1, k5). Repeat to end of round, ending last repeat k3.

Round 34: k3, (m1, k4, m1, k5, m1, k4, m1, k7). Repeat to end of round, ending last repeat k4.

Round 36: (m1, k4, m1, k5, m1, sl 1, k1, psso, k1, k2 tog, m1, k5, m1, k4, m1, k1) to end of round.

Round 38: k1, (m1, k4, m1, k7, m1, sl 1, k2 tog, psso, m1, k7, m1, k4, m1, k3). Repeat to end of round, ending last repeat k2.

Round 40: k2, (m1, k4, m1, k9, m1, k1, m1, k9, m1, k4, m1, k5). Repeat to end of round, ending last repeat k3.

Round 42: k3, (m1, k5, m1, sl 1, k1, psso, k5, k2 tog, m1, k3, m1, sl 1, k1, psso, k5, k2 tog, m1, k5, m1, k7). Repeat to end of round, ending last repeat k4.

Round 44: (m1, k4, m1, k6, m1, sl 1, k1, psso, k3, k2 tog, m1, k5, m1, sl 1, k1, psso, k3, k2 tog, m1, k6, m1, k4, m1, k1) to end of round.

Round 46: k1, [(m1, k5, m1, sl 1, k1, psso, k3, k2 tog, (m1, sl 1, k1, psso, k1, k2 tog, m1, k1) twice, m1, sl 1, k1, psso, k1, k2 tog, m1, sl 1, k1, psso, k3, k2 tog, m1, k5,

m1, k3)]. Repeat to end of round, ending last repeat k2.

Round 48: k2, [(m1, k6, m1, sl 1, k1, psso, k1, k2 tog, m1, k1, (m1, sl 1, k2 tog, psso) 5 times, m1, k1, m1, sl 1, k1, psso, k1, k2 tog, m1, k6, m1, k5)]. Repeat to end of round, ending last repeat k3.

Round 50: k3, [(m1, k7, m1, sl 1, k2 tog, psso, m1, k15, m1, sl 1, k2 tog, psso, (m1, k7) twice)]. Repeat to end of round, ending last repeat k4.

Round 52: [(m1, k4, m1, sl 1, k1, psso, k3, k2 tog, (m1, k2 tog) 5 times, m1, k1, (m1, k2 tog) 5 times, m1, sl 1, k1, psso, k3, k2 tog, m1, k4, m1, k1)]. Repeat to end of round.

Round 54: k1, (m1, k5, m1, sl 1, k1, psso, k1, k2 tog, m1, k23, m1, sl 1, k1, psso, k1, k2 tog, m1, k5, m1, k3). Repeat to end of round, ending last repeat k2.

Round 56: k2, [(m1, k6, m1, sl 1, k2 tog, psso, (m1, k2 tog) 6 times, m1, k1, (m1, k2 tog) 6 times, m1, sl 1, k2 tog, psso, m1, k6, m1, k5)]. Repeat to end of round, ending last repeat k3.

Round 58: k3, (m1, sl 1, k1, psso, k3, k2 tog, m1, k29, m1, sl 1, k1, psso, k3, k2 tog, m1, k7). Repeat to end of round, ending last repeat k4.

Round 60: [(m1, k2 tog) twice, m1, sl 1, k1, psso, k1, k2 tog, (m1, k2 tog) 14 times, m1, k3 tog, m1, sl 1, k1, psso, k1, k2 tog, (m1, k2 tog) twice, m1, k1)]. Repeat to end of round.

Round 62: k5, (m1, sl 1, k2 tog, psso, m1, k31, m1, sl 1, k2 tog, psso, m1, k11). Repeat to end of round, ending last repeat k6.

Cast off knitwise thus:

(Cast on 3 sts, cast off 6 sts, sl remaining st back to LH needle.) Repeat to end.

Fasten off. Darn in end.

Pin out the doily evenly at the six points. Press the work thoroughly to form a true hexagon.

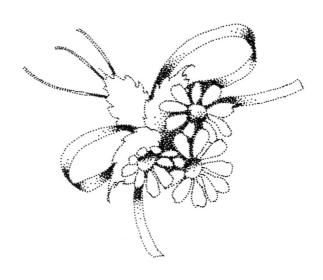

19 BOLERIEN LACE

A Victorian tray cloth trimmed with white cotton embroidery. Bolerien lace was very popular during the Victorian era.

Materials
White traycloth
White DMC cotton, suggested size 20
Needles suggested, 1.25 mm (18)
Sewing thread and needle for attaching lace.
No quantities are given, as these will depend on the knitter's choice of cloth, threads and needles.
Victorian linen can be found in antique centres.

Special abbreviation
inc = k in f&b of st

Cast on 38 sts.
Work 2 foundation rows thus:
Row 1: sl 1, k2, m1, k2 tog, k6, m1, k2 tog, k1, (m1, k2 tog) 6 times, k12.
Row 2: k27, m1, k2 tog, k6, m1, k2 tog, k1.
Continue pattern thus:

Row 1: sl 1, k2, m1, (k2 tog) twice, m2, sl 1, k1, psso, k2, m1, k2 tog, k19, k2 tog, m1, k2 tog, m3, k1, inc.
Row 2: k4, p1, k25, m1, k2 tog, k2, p1, k3, m1, k2 tog, k1.
Row 3: sl 1, k2, m1, k2 tog, k6, m1, k2 tog, k17, k2 tog, (m1, k2 tog) twice, k5.
Row 4: Cast off 2 sts; k26, m1, k2 tog, k6, m1, k2 tog, k1.
Row 5: sl 1, k2, m1, (k2 tog) twice, m2, sl 1, k1, psso, k2, m1, k2 tog, k15, k2 tog, (m1, k2 tog) 3 times, m3, k1, inc.
Row 6: As row 2.
Row 7: sl 1, k2, m1, k2 tog, k6, m1, k2 tog, k13, k2 tog, (m1, k2 tog) 4 times, k5.
Row 8: As row 4.
Row 9: sl 1, k2, m1, (k2 tog) twice, m2, sl 1, k1, psso, k2, m1, k2 tog, k11, k2 tog, (m1, k2 tog) 5 times, m3, k1, inc.
Row 10: As row 2.
Row 11: sl 1, k2, m1, k2 tog, k6, m1, k2 tog, k9, k2 tog, (m1, k2 tog) 6 times, k5.

Row 12: As row 4.

Row 13: sl 1, k2, m1, (k2 tog) twice, m2, sl 1, k1, psso, k2, m1, k2 tog, k7, k2 tog, (m1, k2 tog) 7 times, m3, k1, inc.

Row 14: As row 2.

Row 15: sl 1, k2, m1, k2 tog, k6, m1, k2 tog, k5, k2 tog, (m1, k2 tog) 8 times, k5.

Row 16: As row 4.

Row 17: sl 1, k2, m1, (k2 tog) twice, m2, sl 1, k1, psso, k2, m1, k2 tog, k3, k2 tog, (m1, k2 tog) 9 times, m3, k1, inc.

Row 18: As row 2.

Row 19: sl 1, k2, (m1, k2 tog, k6) twice, (m1, k2 tog) 8 times, k6.

Row 20: Cast off 3 sts, k26, m1, k2 tog, k6, m1, k2 tog, k1.

Row 21: sl 1, k2, m1, (k2 tog) twice, m2, sl 1, k1, psso, k2, m1, k2 tog, k8, (m1, k2 tog) 7 times, m3, k2 tog, inc.

Row 22: As row 2.

Row 23: sl 1, k2, m1, k2 tog, k6, m1, k2 tog, k10, (m1, k2 tog) 6 times, k6.

Row 24: As row 20.

Row 25: sl 1, k2, m1, (m2 tog) twice, m2, sl 1, k1, psso, k2, m1, k2 tog, k12, (m1, k2 tog) 5 times, m3, k2 tog, inc.

Row 26: As row 2.

Row 27: sl 1, k2, m1, k2 tog, k6, m1, k2 tog, k14, (m1, k2 tog) 4 times, k6.

Row 28: As row 20.

Row 29: sl 1, k2, m1, (k2 tog) twice, m2, sl 1, k1, psso, k2, m1, k2 tog, k16, (m1, k2 tog) 3 times, m3, k2 tog, inc.

Row 30: As row 2.

Row 31: sl 1, k2, m1, k2 tog, k6, m1, k2 tog, k18, (m1, k2 tog) twice, k6.

Row 32: As row 20.

Row 33: sl 1, k2, m1, (k2 tog) twice, m2, sl 1, k1, psso, k2, m1, k2 tog, k20, m1, k2 tog, m3, k2 tog, inc.

Row 34: As row 2.

Row 35: sl 1, k2, m1, k2 tog, k6, m1, k2 tog, k1, (m1, k2 tog) 6 times, k15.

Row 36: Cast off 3 sts, k26, m1, k2 tog, k6, m1, k2 tog, k1.

Repeat rows 1–36 until length required to fit the traycloth.

20 ABBEY SQUARE

Abbey Square is a versatile design suitable for a variety of uses, such as a table cloth, shawl, or a small cot covering. A favourite pattern, expertly knitted by Ruth Rintoule, dating from the mid-nineteenth century.

Materials
5 x 50 g balls DMC 10
Needles 2.75 mm (12)
The finished Abbey Square is 76 cm (30″) square.
Use finer DMC threads for a more delicate effect.

CENTRE

Special abbreviations
k3 in next st = (k1, p1, k1) in m1 of previous row
Cast off 3 sts = count the st left on needle

Cast on 171 sts.
Knit 10 rows.
Row 11: k12, (cast off 3 sts, k15) 8 times, cast off 3 sts, k12.
Row 12: k12, (m1, k15) 8 times, m1, k12.
Row 13: k12, (m3 in next st, k15) 8 times, m3, k12.
Row 14: Knit.
Row 15: k9, (cast off 3 sts, k3, cast off 3 sts, k9) 9 times.
Row 16: k9, (m1, k3, m1, k9) 9 times.
Row 17: k9, (m3, k3, m3, k9) 9 times.
Row 18: Knit.
Row 19: k6, (cast off 3 sts, k3) 26 times, cast off 3 sts, k6.
Row 20: k6, (m1, k3) 26 times, m1, k6.
Row 21: k6, (m3, k3) 26 times, m3, k6.
Row 22: Knit.
Row 23: k9, (cast off 3 sts, k9) 9 times.
Row 24: k9, (m1, k3, m1, k9) 9 times.
Row 25: k9, (m3, k3, m3, k9) 9 times.
Row 26: Knit.
Row 27: k12, (cast off 3 sts, k6) 16 times, cast off 3 sts, k12.
Row 28: k12, (m1, k6) 16 times, m1, k12.
Row 29: k12, (m3, k6) 16 times, m3, k12.
Row 30: Knit.
Row 31: k18, (cast off 3 sts, k3, cast off 3 sts, k9) 7 times, cast off 3 sts, k3, cast off 3 sts, k18.
Row 32: k18, (m1, k3, m1, k9) 7 times, m1, k3, m1, k18.
Row 33: k18, (m3, k3, m3, k9) 7 times, m3, k3, m3, k18.
Row 34: Knit.
Row 35: k12, (cast off 3 sts, k6) 16 times, cast off 3 sts, k12.
Row 36: k12, (m1, k6) 16 times, m1, k12.
Row 37: k12, (m3, k6) 16 times, m3, k12.
Row 38: Knit.
Repeat rows 15–38 until length required, ending on row 26.
Then work rows 11, 12, 13.
Knit 10 rows.
Cast off.

INSERTION

Work 4 pieces thus:
Cast on 2 sts.
Row 1: k1, inc (by knitting in b&f of st).
Row 2: k3.
Row 3: sl 1, k1, inc.
Row 4: k4.
Row 5: sl 1, k2, inc.
Row 6: k5.
Row 7: sl 1, k3, inc.
Row 8: k2, m1, k2 tog, k2.
Row 9: sl 1, k3, m1, k2.
Row 10: k3, m1, k2 tog, k2.
Row 11: sl 1, k3, m1, k2 tog, inc.
Row 12: k4, m1, k2 tog, k2.
Row 13: sl 1, k3, m1, k2 tog, k1, inc.
Row 14: k5, m1, k2 tog, k2.
Row 15: sl 1, k3, m1, k2 tog, k2, inc.
Row 16: k6, m1, k2 tog, k2.
Row 17: sl 1, k3, m1, k2 tog, k3, inc.
Row 18: k7, m1, k2 tog, k2.
Row 19: sl 1, k3, m1, k2 tog, k4, inc.
Row 20: k8, m1, k2 tog, k2.
Row 21: sl 1, k3, m1, k2 tog, k2. Cast off 3 sts, inc in last st.
Row 22: k3, m1, k4, m1, k2 tog, k2.
Row 23: sl 1, k3, m1, k2 tog, k2, m3, k2, inc.
Row 24: k11, m1, k2 tog, k2.
Row 25: sl 1, k3, m1, k2 tog, k5, cast off 2 sts, inc.
Row 26: k3, m1, k7, m1, k2 tog, k2.
Row 27: sl 1, k3, m1, k2 tog, k5, m3, k2, inc.
Row 28: k14, m1, k2 tog, k2.
Row 29: sl 1, k3, m1, k2 tog, cast off 3 sts, k3, cast off 3 sts, inc in last st.
Row 30: k3, m1, k3, m1, k4, m1, k2 tog, k2.
Row 31: sl 1, k3, m1, k2 tog, k2, m3, k3, m3, k2, inc.
Row 32: k17, m1, k2 tog, k2.
Row 33: sl 1, k3, m1, k2 tog, k5, cast off 3 sts, k5, inc.
Row 34: k8, m1, k7, m1, k2 tog, k2.
Row 35: sl 1, k3, m1, k2 tog, k5, m3, k7, inc.
Row 36: k19, m1, k2 tog, k2.
Row 37: sl 1, k3, m1, k2 tog, k2, (cast off 3 sts, k3) twice, m1, k2 tog, inc.
Row 38: sl 1, k3, m1, k2 tog, k1, m1, k3, m1, k4, m1, k2 tog, k2.
Row 39: sl 1, k3, m1, k2 tog, k2, (m3, k3) twice, m1, k2 tog, k1, inc.
Row 40: sl 1, k3, m1, k2 tog, k15, m1, k2 tog, k2.
This completes the 1st corner.

Continue thus for straight insertion:
Row 1: sl 1, k3, m1, k2 tog, k5, cast off 3 sts, k7, m1, k2 tog, k2.

Row 2: sl 1, k3, m1, k2 tog, k5, m1, k7, m1, k2 tog, k2.
Row 3: sl 1, k3, m1, k2 tog, k5, m3, k7, m1, k2 tog, k2.
Row 4: sl 1, k3, m1, k2 tog, k15, m1, k2 tog, k2.
Row 5: sl 1, k3, m1, k2 tog, k2, cast off 3 sts, k3, cast off 3 sts, k4, m1, k2 tog, k2.
Row 6: sl 1, k3, m1, k2 tog, k2, m1, k3, m1, k4, m1, k2 tog, k2.
Row 7: sl 1, k3, m1, k2 tog, k2, m3, k3, m3, k4, m1, k2 tog, k2.
Row 8: sl 1, k3, m1, k2 tog, k15, m1, k2 tog, k2.
Repeat rows 1–8 for length required.

Work 2nd corner thus:
Row 1: sl 1, k3, m1, k2 tog, k5, cast off 3 sts, k6, m1, k2 tog, k2.
Row 2: sl 1, k1, psso, k2, m1, k2 tog, k5, m1, k7, m1, k2 tog, k2.
Row 3: sl 1, k3, m1, k2 tog, k5, m3, k7, m1, k2 tog, k1.
Row 4: sl 1, k1, psso, k1, m1, k2 tog, k15, m1, k2 tog, k2.
Row 5: sl 1, k3, m1, k2 tog, k2. Cast off 3 sts, k3, cast off 3 sts, k4, m1, k2 tog.
Row 6: sl 1, k1, psso, k2 tog, k2, m1, k3, m1, k4, m1, k2 tog, k2.
Row 7: sl 1, k3, m1, k2 tog, k2, m3, k3, m3, k2, k2 tog.
Row 8: sl 1, k1, psso, k4, m1, k2 tog, k2.
Row 9: sl 1, k3, m1, k2 tog, k5. Cast off 3 sts, k3, k2 tog.
Row 10: sl 1, k1, psso, k2, m1, k7, m1, k2 tog, k2.
Row 11: sl 1, k3, m1, k2 tog, k5, m3, k3.
Row 12: sl 1, k1, psso, k11, m1, k2 tog, k2.
Row 13: sl 1, k3, m1, k2 tog, k2. Cast off 3 sts, k3, k2 tog.
Row 14: sl 1, k1, psso, k2, m1, k4, m1, k2 tog, k2.
Row 15: sl 1, k3, m1, k2 tog, k2, m3, k1, k2 tog.
Row 16: sl 1, k1, psso, k7, m1, k2 tog, k2.
Row 17: sl 1, k3, m1, k2 tog, k6.
Row 18: sl 1, k1, psso, k6, m1, k2 tog, k2.
Row 19: sl 1, k3, m1, k2 tog, k5.
Row 20: sl 1, k1, psso, k5, m1, k2 tog, k2.
Row 21: sl 1, k3, m1, k2 tog, k4.
Row 22: sl 1, k1, psso, k4, m1, k2 tog, k2.
Row 23: sl 1, k3, m1, k2 tog, k3.
Row 24: sl 1, k1, psso, k3, m1, k2 tog, k2.
Row 25: sl 1, k3, m1, k2 tog, k2.
Row 26: sl 1, k1, psso, k2, m1, k2 tog, k2.
Row 27: sl 1, k3, m1, k2 tog, k1.
Row 28: sl 1, k1, psso, k1, m1, k2 tog, k2.
Row 29: sl 1, k3, k2 tog.
Row 30: sl 1, k1, psso, k3.
Row 31: sl 1, k1, k2 tog.
Row 32: Cast off.

LACE EDGING

Work 1st half of corner thus:
Cast on 4 sts.
Knit 4 rows.
Row 1: Cast on 3 sts, k3 cast off 3 sts.
Row 2: Cast on 3 sts, k4, m1, k3.
Row 3: k3, m3, k4.
Row 4: k10.
Row 5: Cast on 3 sts, (k3, cast off 3 sts) twice.
Row 6: Cast on 3 sts, k4, (m1, k3) twice.
Row 7: (k3, m3) twice, k4.
Row 8: k16.
Row 9: (cast off 3 sts, k3) twice, cast off 3 sts.
Row 10: Cast on 3 sts, k4, (m1, k3) twice.
Row 11: (k3, m3) twice, k4.
Row 12: k16.
Row 13: (cast off 3 sts, k3) twice, cast off 3 sts.
Row 14: Cast on 3 sts, k4, (m1, k3) twice.
Row 15: (k3, m3) twice, k4.
Row 16: k16.
Row 17: (cast off 3 sts, k3) twice, cast off 3 sts.
Row 18: Cast on 3 sts, k4, (m1, k3) twice.
Row 19: (k3, m3) twice, k4.
Row 20: Cast on 1 st, knit to end of row (17 sts).
Row 21: (cast off 3 sts, k3) twice, cast off 3 sts, inc in last st (NB: inc = purl in b&f of st).
Row 22: Cast on 1 st, k4, (m1, k3) twice.
Row 23: (k3, m3) twice, k3, inc.
Row 24: Cast on 2 sts, knit to end of row (19 sts).
Row 25: Cast on 3 sts, k3, (cast off 3 sts, k3) 3 times, inc.
Row 26: k5, (m1, k3) 3 times.
Row 27: (k3, m3) 3 times, k5.
Row 28: Cast on 1 st, k24.

Commence straight lace thus:
Row 1: Cast on 3 sts, (k3, cast off 3 sts) 3 times, k9.
Row 2: k9, (m1, k3) 3 times.
Row 3: (k3, m3) 3 times, k9.
Row 4: Knit (27 sts).
Row 5: Cast on 3 sts, (k3, cast off 3 sts) 3 times, k12.
Row 6: k12, (m1, k3) 3 times.
Row 7: (k3, m3) 3 times, k12.
Row 8: Knit (30 sts).
Row 9: Cast on 3 sts, (k3, cast off 3 sts) 3 times, k15.
Row 10: k15, (m1, k3) 3 times.
Row 11: (k3, m3) 3 times, k15.
Row 12: Knit (33 sts).
Row 13: (cast off 3 sts, k3) 3 times, cast off 3 sts, k12.
Row 14: k12, (m1, k3) 3 times.
Row 15: (k3, m3) 3 times, k12.
Row 16: Knit (30 sts).
Row 17: (cast off 3 sts, k3) 3 times, cast off 3 sts, k9.
Row 18: k9, (m1, k3) 3 times.

Row 19: (k3, m3) 3 times, k9.
Row 20: Knit (27 sts).
Row 21: (cast off 3 sts, k3) 3 times, cast off 3 sts, k6.
Row 22: k6, (m1, k3) 3 times.
Row 23: (k3, m3) 3 times, k6.
Row 24: Knit (24 sts).
Repeat rows 1–24 until length required, ending with row 16.

Commence 2nd half of corner thus:
Row 1: (cast off 3 sts, k3) 4 times, k8.
Row 2: sl 1, k1, psso, k7, (m1, k3) 3 times.
Row 3: (k3, m3) 3 times, k8.
Row 4: sl 1, k1, psso, k to end of row.
Row 5: (cast off 3 sts, k3) 4 times, cast off 3 sts, k4.
Row 6: sl 1, k1, psso, k2, (m1, k3) 3 times.
Row 7: (k3, m3) 3 times, k3.
Row 8: sl 1, k1, psso. knit to end of row.
Row 9: (cast off 3 sts, k3) 3 times, k2.
Row 10: k5, (m1, k3) 3 times.
Row 11: (k3, m3) twice, k5.
Row 12: Cast off 3 sts, knit to end of row.
Row 13: Cast on 3 sts, (k3, cast off 3 sts) twice, k4.
Row 14: k5, (m1, k3) twice.
Row 15: (k3, m3) twice, k5.

Row 16: Cast off 3 sts, knit to end of row.
Row 17: Cast on 3 sts, (k3, cast off 3 sts) twice, k4.
Row 18: Cast off 3 sts, k1, (m1, k3) twice.
Row 19: (k3, m3) twice, k2.
Row 20: Cast off 3 sts, knit to end of row.
Row 21: Cast on 3 sts, (k3, cast off 3 sts) twice, k1.
Row 22: k2, (m1, k3) twice.
Row 23: (k3, m3) twice, k2.
Row 24: Cast off 2 sts, knit to end of row (12 sts).
Row 25: Cast on 3 sts, (k3, cast off 3 sts) twice, k2.
Row 26: (k3, m1) twice, k3.
Row 27: (k3, m3) twice, k3.
Row 28: Cast off 3 sts, knit to end of row.
Row 29: Cast off 3 sts, k3, cast off 3 sts, k2.
Row 30: k3, m1, k3.
Row 31: k3, m3, k3.
Row 32: Cast off 3 sts, knit to end of row.
Row 33: As row 32.
Row 34: Knit.
Cast off.

To make up
Press the cloth if necessary. Join insertion corners and attach to centre square, then join edging corners and attach to insertion.

21 LISETTE

A rose-leaf panelled gown, beautifully knitted by Edna Lomas. Lisette is a modern 1985 Hillview Lane Limited Edition 61 cm (24") doll. Nina, the doll in the black gown, is a reproduction by Ria Warke. Lisette comes from the author's collection.

Materials
3 x 50 g balls DMC 20 cotton
Needles 2.75 mm (12); for bodice 2 mm (14)

Front of dress

Cast on 163 sts.
Knit 3 rows.
Row 1: **k3, *m1, k5, m1, sl 1, k2 tog, psso, m1, sl 1, k1, psso, sl 1, k2 tog, psso, (k1, m1) twice, k3. Repeat from * to last 16 sts. M1, k5, m1, sl 1, k2 tog, psso, m1, sl 1, k1, psso, sl 1, k2 tog, psso, (k1, m1) twice, k1.
Row 2 and alternate rows: k1, *p15, k3. Repeat from * to end of row.
Row 3: k3, *m1, k2, sl 1, k2 tog, psso, k2, m1, sl 1, k1, psso, m1, sl 1, k2 tog, psso, (m1, k3) twice. Repeat from * to last 16 sts, m1, k2, sl 1, k2 tog, psso, k2, m1, sl 1, k1, psso, m1, k1, k2 tog, psso, m1, k3, m1, k1.
Row 5: k3, *(m1, k1) twice, sl 1, k2 tog, psso, k2 tog, m1, sl 1, k2 tog, psso, m1, k5, m1, k3. Repeat from * to last 16 sts, (m1, k1) twice, sl 1, k2 tog, psso, k2 tog, m1, sl 1, k2 tog, psso, m1, k5, m1, k1.
Row 7: k36, [(k3, m1) twice, sl 1, k2 tog, psso, m1, k2 tog, m1, k2, sl 1, k2 tog, psso, k2, m1, k18)] 3 times, k19.
Row 8: As row 2**
Repeat from **–** 4 times.

Proceed as follows:
Row 1: ***k36, [(k3, m1, k5, m1, sl 1, k2 tog, psso, m1, sl 1, k1, psso, sl 1, k2 tog, psso, (k1, m1) twice, k18)] 3 times, k19.
Row 2 and alternate rows: k1, *p15, k3. Repeat from * to end of row.
Row 3: k36, (k3, m1, k2, sl 1, k2 tog, psso, k2, m1, sl 1, k1, psso, m1, sl 1, k2 tog, psso, m1, k3, m1, k18) 3 times, k19.
Row 5: k36, [(k3, (m1, k1) twice, sl 1, k2 tog, psso, k2 tog, m1, sl 1, k2 tog, psso, m1, k5, m1, k18)] 3 times, k19.
Row 7: k36, [(k3, m1) twice, sl 1, k2 tog, psso, m1, k2 tog, m1, k2, sl 1, k2 tog, psso, k2, m1, k18)] 3 times, k19.
Row 8: As row 2***
Repeat ***–*** 11 times.

To work bodice, change to 2 mm (14) needles.
Proceed as follows:
Row 1: (k2 tog) 18 times, *k3, m1, k5, m1, sl 1, k2 tog, psso, m1, sl 1, k1, psso, sl 1, k2 tog, psso, (k1, m1) twice, k3*, (k2 tog) 25 times, k1. Repeat *–* once, (k2 tog) 17 times.
Row 2: k1, p16, k3, p15, k3, p26, k3, p15, k3, p17, k1.
Row 3: (k1, k2 tog) 6 times, *k3, m1, k2, sl 1, k2 tog, psso, k2, m1, sl 1, k1, psso, m1, sl 1, k2 tog, psso, (m1, k3) twice*, (k2 tog) 13 times. Repeat from *–* once, (k2 tog, k1) 5 times, k2 (79sts).
Row 4 and alternate rows: k1, p11, k3, p15, k3, p13, k3, p15, k3, p11, k1.
Row 5: k12, *k3, (m1, k1) twice, sl 1, k2 tog, psso, k2 tog, m1, sl 1, k2 tog, psso, m1, k5, m1, k3*, k13. Repeat from *–* once, k12.
Row 7: k12, *(k3, m1) twice, sl 1, k2 tog, psso, m1, k2 tog, m1, k2, sl 1, k2 tog, psso, k2, m1, k3*, k13. Repeat from *–* once, k12.
Row 9: k12, *k3, m1, k5, m1, sl 1, k2 tog, psso, m1, sl 1, k1, psso, sl 1, k2 tog, psso, (k1, m1) twice, k3*, k13. Repeat *–* once, k12.
Row 11: k12, *k3, m1, k2, sl 1, k2 tog, psso, k2, m1, sl 1, k1, psso, m1, sl 1, k2 tog, psso, (m1, k3) twice*, k13. Repeat *–* once, k12.
Row 12: As row 4.

Proceed as follows:
Cast off 5 sts at beginning of next 2 rows.
Next row: k2 tog, work 31 sts in pattern, k2 tog, turn.
Continue working in pattern. Dec once at armhole edge in every alternate row 3 times (30 sts).
Work 22 rows in pattern without shaping.
Cast off 6 sts at beginning of next row.
Dec once at neck edge in every row until 20 sts remain.
Work 6 rows without shaping.
Cast off.
Join the yarn where the sts were left. Work other side to correspond.

Back of dress

Using 2.75 mm (12) needles, work as for front until there are 79 sts on needle.

Work 9 rows in pattern without shaping.

Cast off 5 sts at the beginning of each of the next 2 rows.

Dec once at each end of the needle in the next and every alternate row 4 times (61 sts).

Continue working in pattern without shaping until the armhole measures the same as front armhole.

Cast off.

Sleeves (make 2)

Using 2 mm (14) needles cast on 42 sts.

Work in k1, p1 rib for 25 cm (1").

Next row: Work row of ribbon holes thus: k2, (m1, k2 tog, k1) to end of row.

Next row: Knit.

Next row: Purl.

Next row: k6, *inc once in next st, repeat from * to last 5 sts, k5 (73 sts).

Next row: Purl.

Change to 2.75 mm (12) needles. Proceed as follows:

Continue in pattern as given for front, from **–** once.

Work in st, st for 15 cm (6") or length required.

Cast off.

Lace for neck

Cast on 8 sts.

Row 1: k1, k2 tog, m2, k2 tog, k1, m4, k2.

Row 2: k2, (k1, p1) twice in m4 of previous row, k3, p1, k2.

Rows 3 and 4: k12.

Row 5: k1, k2 tog, m2, k2 tog, k1, (m2, k2 tog) 3 times.

Row 6: (k2, p1) 3 times, k3, p1, k2.

Row 7: k15.

Row 8: Cast off 7 sts, k7.

Repeat rows 1–8 until length required.

To make up

Press the pieces of the dress under a damp cloth, taking care not to flatten the decorative panels. Join side, shoulder and sleeve seams. Sew sleeves into armholes, adjusting any fullness at the top of sleeves. Using crochet hook work one row dc around front opening. Then work row of loops down each side of opening. Lace together with fine cord.

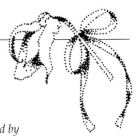

22 LEAH

Blanket edging by Ruth Rintoule. Sleep sachet by Joan Eckersley. Pomander, knitted by author and embroidered by Joan Jackson, on a bedspread knitted by author. Antique bear is Uther from author's collection.

Materials
1 x 50 g ball DMC Hermina
Needles 2 mm (14)

Cast on 19 sts.
Row 1: m1, k2 tog. K to last 3 sts, m1, k2 tog, k1.
Row 2: k2, m1, k2 tog, k3, (m1, p2 tog) twice, p1, k5, m1, k2.
Row 3 and alternate rows: As row 1.
Row 4: k2, m1, k2 tog, k2, (m1, p2 tog) 3 times, p1, k5, m1, k2.
Row 6: k2, m1, k2 tog, k1, (m1, p2 tog) 4 times, p1, k5, m1, k2.
Row 8: k2, m1, k2 tog, (m1, p2 tog) 5 times, p1, k5, m1, k2.

Row 10: k2, m1, k2 tog, k1, (m1, p2 tog) 4 times, p1, k4, k2 tog, m1, k2 tog, k1.
Row 12: k2, m1, k2 tog, k2, (m1, p2 tog) 3 times, p1, k4, k2 tog, m1, p2 tog, k1.
Row 14: k2, m1, k2 tog, k3, (m1, p2 tog) twice, p1, k4, k2 tog, m1, p2 tog, k1.
Row 16: k2, m1, k2 tog, k4, m1, p2 tog, p1, k4, k2 tog, m1, k2 tog, k1.
Repeat rows 1–16 until length desired ending with row 1.
Cast off.
Press lightly. Sew edging to blanket.

23 POMANDER

A decorative pomander knitted by the author, and embroidered by Joan Jackson.

Materials
1 x 20 g ball DMC 20 cotton
Needles 1.25 mm (18)
DMC embroidery threads
Tassel made from stranded embroidery cotton to match embroidery
Colours used by Joan are the same as the colours used in Amy Rose (221, 223, 224, 225, 501, 502, 522).

Cast on 40 sts.
Row 1: k to last st, turn
Row 2: sl 1, k to last st, turn.

Rows 3 and 4: k to last 2 sts, turn.
Rows 5 and 6: k to last 3 sts, turn.
Continue working this way until 10 sts remain at both ends of row. K to end of row.
Repeat until 8 sections are completed.
Cast off.

Fill the pomander with soft fibre to which you have added potpourri. Close the seam as neatly as possible. Embroider with flowers, add a small tassel. Knit a small length of cord to hang the pomander, if desired.

24 SLEEP SACHET

Joan Eckersley designed and knitted a sleep sachet in a simple and elegant shape. These sachets are tucked under the pillow, where the warmth of the bed releases the aroma of the herbs, encouraging relaxation.

Materials
2 x 20 g balls DMC Cébélia 20
Needles 1.75 mm (15)
Sleep sachet measures 14 cm x 21.5 cm (5½″ x 8½″)

Cast on 79 sts.
Row 1: Knit.
Row 2: Purl.
Row 3: k2, purl to last 2 sts, k2.
Work in pattern thus:
Row 1: k3, (m1, sl 1, k1, psso, k1, m1, k2 tog, k1) 12 times, m1, sl 1, k1, psso, k2.
Row 2 and alternate rows: k2, purl to last 2 sts, k2.
Row 3: k4, (m1, sl 1, k1, psso, k1, k2 tog, m1, k1) 12 times, k3.
Row 5: k5, (m1, sl 1, k2 tog, psso, m1, k3) 12 times, k2.
Row 7: k3, (m1, k2 tog, k1, m1, sl 1, k1, psso, k1) 12 times, m1, k2 tog, k2.
Row 9: k3, k2 tog, m1, (k3, m1, sl 1, k2 tog, psso, m1) 11 times, k3, m1, sl 1, k1, psso, k3.
Row 10: k2, purl to last 2 sts, k2.
Repeat rows 1–10 until length desired.
Knit 2 rows.
Cast off.

Edging
Cast on 12 sts.
Knit 1 row.
Row 1: sl 1, k1, m1, k2 tog, k1, m2, k2 tog, k5.
Row 2: sl 1, k6, p1, k5.
Row 3: sl 1, k1, m1, k2 tog, k9.
Row 4: sl 1, k12.
Row 5: sl 1, k1, m1, k2 tog, k1, m2, k2 tog, m2, k6.
Row 6: sl 1, k6, p1, k2, p1, k5.
Row 7: sl 1, k1, m1, k2 tog, k12.
Row 8: Cast off 4 sts, k11.
Repeat rows 1–8 until lace is long enough to edge sachet, allowing ample fullness at each corner.

To make up
Make a fine cotton envelope-style sachet. Attach the knitted sachet cover to the top of the fabric sachet. Fill sachet with fibre filling, mixed with aromatic dried herbs. Tuck sachets under pillows for a restful sleep. Sleep sachets can be decorated with embroidery or ribbons. They make an excellent gift.

25 LANCEFIELD LACE

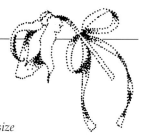

Ruth Rintoule of Lalor, Victoria, knitted the lace for this beautiful special occasion cloth, with twelve formal size matching napkins.
The pattern dates from the nineteenth century, and has an elegant charm. Ruth's Lancefield Lace cloth will be a Rintoule family heirloom, a tribute to a master knitter. We are fortunate to include it in this book.
Lancefield Lace could enhance many household items, especially napery and towels.

Materials
12 x 50 g balls DMC Cébélia 20 cotton
Needles 2 mm (14)
Plain white tablecloth of size desired

TABLECLOTH LACE

Special abbreviation:
inc in this pattern = k into b&f of st

First half corner

Cast on 2 sts.
Row 1: m1, k2.
Row 2: m1, k2 tog, inc in last st.
Row 3: k4.
Row 4: m1, k2 tog, k1, m1, inc in last st.
Row 5: k6.
Row 6: m1, k2 tog, k1, m1, k2 tog, m1, inc in last st.
Row 7: k8.
Row 8: m1, k2 tog, k1, (m1, k2 tog) twice, m1, inc in last st.
Row 9: k10.
Row 10: m1, k2 tog, k1, (m1, k2 tog) 3 times, m1, inc in last st.
Row 11: k12.
Row 12: m1, k2 tog, k1, (m1, k2 tog) 4 times, m1, inc in last st.
Row 13: k14.
Row 14: m1, k2 tog, k1, (m1, k2 tog) 5 times, m1, inc in last st.
Row 15: k16.
Row 16: m1, k2 tog, k1, (m1, k2 tog) 6 times, m1, inc in last st.
Row 17: k18.
Row 18: m1, k2 tog, k15, inc in last st.
Row 19: s1, k1, (m1, k2 tog) 7 times, m1, k3 (20 sts).
Row 20: m1, k2 tog, k17, inc in last st.
Row 21: k21.
Row 22: m1, (k2 tog) twice, (m1, k2 tog) 7 times, k2, inc in last st.

Row 23: Knit.
Row 24: m1, (k2 tog) twice, (m1, k2 tog) 6 times, k4, m1, k1.
Row 25: s1, k1, m1, k2 tog, k17.
Row 26: m1, (k2 tog) twice, (m1, k2 tog) 5 times, k5, m1, k2.
Row 27: s1, k1, m1, k2 tog, k16.
Row 28: m1, (k2 tog) twice, (m1, k2 tog) 4 times, k6, m1, k2 tog, inc in last st.
Row 29: k4, m1, k2 tog, k15.
Row 30: m1, (k2 tog) twice, (m1, k2 tog) 3 times, k7, m1, k2 tog, k1, m1, k1.
Row 31: k5, m1, k2 tog, k14.
Row 32: m1, (k2 tog) twice, (m1, k2 tog) twice, k8, m1, k2 tog, k1, m1, k2.
Row 33: k6, m1, k2 tog, k13.
Row 34: m1, (k2 tog) twice, m1, k2 tog, k9, m1, k2 tog, k1, m1, k2 tog, inc in last st.
Row 35: k7, m1, k2 tog, k12.
Row 36: m1, (k2 tog) twice, m1, k10, (m1, k2 tog, k1) twice, inc in last st.
Row 37: k8, m1, k2 tog, k12.
Row 38: m1, k2 tog, k1, m1, k2 tog, m1, k9, m1, k2 tog, k1, m1, k2 tog, k2, inc in last st.
Row 39: k9, m1, k2 tog, k13.
Row 40: m1, k2 tog, k1, (m1, k2 tog) twice, m1, k8, m1, k2 tog, k1, m1, k2 tog, k3, inc in last st.
Row 41: k10, m1, k2 tog, k14.
Row 42: m1, k2 tog, k1, (m1, k2 tog) 3 times, m1, k7, m1, k2 tog, k1, m1, k2 tog, k4, m1, k1.
Row 43: k11, m1, k2 tog, k15.
Row 44: m1, k2 tog, k1, (m1, k2 tog) 4 times, m1, k6, m1, k2 tog, k1, m1, k2 tog, k3, k2 tog, m1, inc in last st.
Row 45: k12, m1, k2 tog, k16.
Row 46: m1, k2 tog, k1, (m1, k2 tog) 5 times, m1, k5, m1, k2 tog, k1, m1, k2 tog, k3, k2 tog, m1, k1, inc in last st.
Row 47: k13, m1, k2 tog, k17.
Row 48: m1, k2 tog, k1, (m1, k2 tog) 6 times, m1, k4, m1, k2 tog, k2, m1, k2 tog, k1, k2 tog, m1, k3, inc in last st.
Row 49: k14, m1, k2 tog, k18.
Row 50: m1, k2 tog, k18, m1, k2 tog, k3, m1, s1, k2 tog, psso, m1, k5, inc in last st.
Row 51: s1, k1, m1, k2 tog, k11, m1, k2 tog, k1, (m1, k2 tog) 7 times, m1, k3.

Row 52: m1, k2 tog, k19, m1, k2 tog, k4, m1, k1, m1, k6, m1, k2.

Row 53: s1, k2, m1, k2 tog, k13, m1, k2 tog, k19.

Row 54: m1, (k2 tog) twice, (m1, k2 tog) 7 times, k3, m1, k2 tog, k2, k2 tog, m1, k3, m1, k2 tog, k4, m1, k2 tog, k1.

Row 55: s1, k2, m1, k2 tog, k13, m1, k2 tog, k18.

Row 56: m1, (k2 tog) twice, (m1, k2 tog) 6 times, k4, m1, k2 tog, k1, k2 tog, m1, k2 tog, m1, k1, (m1, k2 tog) twice, k3, m1, k2 tog, k1.

Row 57: s1, k2, m1, k2 tog, k13, m1, k2 tog, k17.

Row 58: m1, (k2 tog) twice, (m1, k2 tog) 5 times, k5, m1, (k2 tog) twice, m1, k2 tog, m1, k3, (m1, k2 tog) twice, k2, m1, k2 tog, k1.

Row 59: s1, k2, m1, k2 tog, k13, m1, k2 tog, k16.

Row 60: m1, (k2 tog) twice, (m1, k2 tog) 4 times, k6, m1, k2 tog, k1, (m1, k2 tog) twice, k1, (k2 tog, m1) twice, k3, m1, k2 tog, k1.

Row 61: s1, k2, m1, k2 tog, k13, m1, k2 tog, k15.

Row 62: m1, (k2 tog) twice, (m1, k2 tog) 3 times, k7, m1, k2 tog, k2, m1, k2 tog, m1, s1, k2 tog, psso, m1, k2 tog, m1, k4, m1, k2 tog, k1.

Row 63: s1, k2, m1, k2 tog, k13, m1, k2 tog, k14.

Row 64: m1, (k2 tog) twice, (m1, k2 tog) twice, k8, m1, k2 tog, k3, m1, k2 tog, k1, k2 tog, m1, k5, m1, k2 tog, k1.

Row 65: s1, k2, (m1, k2 tog, k13) twice.

Row 66: m1, (k2 tog) twice, m1, k2 tog, k9, m1, k2 tog, k4, m1, s1, k2 tog, psso, m1, k6, m1, k2 tog, k1.

Row 67: s1, k2, m1, k2 tog, k13, m1, k2 tog, k12.

Row 68: m1, (k2 tog) twice, m1, k10, m1, k2 tog, k3, k2 tog, m1, k1, m1, k2 tog, k5, m1, k2 tog, k1.

Straight lace

Row 1: **s1, k2, m1, k2 tog, k13, m1, k2 tog, k12.

Row 2: m1, k2 tog, k1, m1, k2 tog, m1, k9, m1, k2 tog, k2, k2 tog, m1, k3, m1, k2 tog, k4, m1, k2 tog, k1.

Row 3: s1, k2, (m1, k2 tog, k13) twice.

Row 4: m1, k2 tog, k1, (m1, k2 tog) twice, m1, k8, m1, k2 tog, k1, (k2 tog) twice, k1, (m1, k2 tog) twice, k3, m1, k2 tog, k1.

Row 5: s1, k2, m1, k2 tog, k13, m1, k2 tog, k14.

Row 6: m1, k2 tog, k1, (m1, k2 tog) 3 times, m1, k7, m1, (k2 tog) twice, m1, k2 tog, m1, k3, (m1, k2 tog) twice, k2, m1, k2 tog, k1.

Row 7: s1, k2, m1, k2 tog, k13, m1, k2 tog, k15.

Row 8: m1, k2 tog, k1, (m1, k2 tog) 4 times, m1, k6, m1, k2 tog, k1, (m1, k2 tog) twice, k1, k2 tog, m1, k2 tog, m1, k3, m1, k2 tog, k1.

Row 9: s1, k2, m1, k2 tog, k13, m1, k2 tog, k16.

Row 10: m1, k2 tog, k1, (m1, k2 tog) 5 times, m1, k5, m1, k2 tog, k2, m1, k2 tog, m1, s1, k2 tog, psso, m1, k2 tog, m1, k4, m1, k2 tog, k1.

Row 11: s1, k2, m1, k2 tog, k13, m1, k2 tog, k17.

Row 12: m1, k2 tog, k1, (m1, k2 tog) 6 times, m1, k4, m1,

k2 tog, k3, m1, k2 tog, k1, k2 tog, m1, k5, m1, k2 tog, k1.

Row 13: s1, k2, m1, k2 tog, k13, m1, k2 tog, k18*

Row 14: m1, k2 tog, k18, m1, k2 tog, k4, m1, s1, k2 tog, psso, m1, k6, m1, k2 tog, k1.

Row 15: s1, k2, m1, k2 tog, k13, m1, k2 tog, k1, (m1, k2 tog) 7 times, m1, k3 (39 sts).

Row 16: m1, k2 tog, k19, m1, k2 tog, k3, k2 tog, m1, k1, m1, k2 tog, k5, m1, k2 tog, k1

Now work rows 53–68 inclusive. This completes one lace pattern**

Repeat from row 1 of straight lace pattern ** to ** for length required.

Work second mitre thus:

Work rows 1–13 inclusive ** to *

Continue:

Row 14: m1, k2 tog, k18, m1, k2 tog, k2, k2 tog, m1, s1, k2 tog, psso, m1, k2 tog, k4, m1, k2 tog, k1.

Row 15: s1, k2, m1, k2 tog, k11, m1, k2 tog, k1, (m1, k2 tog) 7 times, m1, k3.

Row 16: m1, k2 tog, k19, m1, k2 tog, k2, k2 tog, m1, k1, m1, k2 tog, k4, m1, k2 tog, k1.

Row 17: s1, k1, psso, k1, m1, k2 tog, k11, m1, k2 tog, k19.

Row 18: m1, (k2 tog) twice, (m1, k2 tog) 7 times, k3, m1, k2 tog, k1, k2 tog, m1, k3, m1, k2 tog, k3, m1, k2 tog.

Row 19: s1, k1, psso, k13, m1, k2 tog, k18.

Row 20: m1, (k2 tog) twice, (m1, k2 tog) 6 times, k4, m1, (k2 tog) twice, m1, k5, m1, k2 tog, k3.

Row 21: s1, k1, psso, k12, m1, k2 tog, k17.

Row 22: m1, (k2 tog) twice, (m1, k2 tog) 5 times, k5, m1, k2 tog, k1, m1, k2 tog, k3, k2 tog, m1, k3.

Row 23: s1, k1, psso, k11, m1, k2 tog, k16.

Row 24: m1, (k2 tog) twice, (m1, k2 tog) 4 times, k6, m1, k2 tog, k1, m1, k2 tog, k3, k2 tog, m1, k2 tog.

Row 25: s1, k10, m1, k2 tog, k15.

Row 26: m1, (k2 tog) twice, (m1, k2 tog) 3 times, k7, m1, k2 tog, k1, m1, k2 tog, k3, k2 tog, k1.

Row 27: s1, k9, m1, k2 tog, k14.

Row 28: m1, (k2 tog) twice, (m1, k2 tog) twice, k8, m1, k2 tog, k1, m1, k2 tog, k3, k2 tog.

Row 29: s1, k8, m1, k2 tog, k13.

Row 30: m1, (k2 tog) twice, m1, k2 tog, k9, (m1, k2 tog, k1) twice, k2 tog, k1.

Row 31: s1, k7, m1, k2 tog, k12.

Row 32: m1, (k2 tog) twice, m1, k10, m1, k2 tog, k1, m1, (k2 tog) twice, k1.

Row 33: s1, k6, m1, k2 tog, k12.

Row 34: m1, k2 tog, k1, m1, k2 tog, m1, k9, m1, k2 tog, k1, m1, (k2 tog) twice.

Row 35: s1, k5, m1, k2 tog, k13.

Row 36: m1, k2 tog, k1, (m1, k2 tog) twice, m1, k8, m1, k2 tog, k1, k3 tog.

Row 37: s1, k4, m1, k2 tog, k14.

Row 38: m1, k2 tog, k1, (m1, k2 tog) 3 times, m1, k7, m1, k2 tog, k1, k2 tog.
Row 39: s1, k3, m1, k2 tog, k15.
Row 40: m1, k2 tog, k1, (m1, k2 tog) 4 times, m1, k6, m1, (k2 tog) twice.
Row 41: s1, k2, m1, k2 tog, k16.
Row 42: m1, k2 tog, k1, (m1, k2 tog) 5 times, m1, k5, m1, k3 tog.
Row 43: s1, k1, m1, k2 tog, k17.
Row 44: m1, k2 tog, k1, (m1, k2 tog) 6 times, m1, k4, k2 tog.
Row 45: s1, k1, psso, k19.
Row 46: m1, k2 tog, k16, k2 tog.
Row 47: s1, k1, (m1, k2 tog) 7 times, m1, k3.
Row 48: m1, k2 tog, k16, k2 tog.
Row 49: s1, k1, psso, k17.
Row 50: m1, (k2 tog) twice, (m1, k2 tog) 7 times.
Row 51: s1, k1, psso, k15.
Row 52: m1, (k2 tog) twice, (m1, k2 tog) 6 times.
Row 53: s1, k1, psso, k13.
Row 54: m1, (k2 tog) twice, (m1, k2 tog) 5 times.
Row 55: s1, k1, psso, k11.
Row 56: m1, (k2 tog) twice, (m1, k2 tog) 4 times.
Row 57: s1, k1, psso, k9.
Row 58: m1, (k2 tog) twice, (m1, k2 tog) 3 times.
Row 59: s1, k1, psso, k7.
Row 60: m1, (k2 tog) twice, (m1, k2 tog) twice.
Row 61: s1, k1, psso, k5.
Row 62: m1, (k2 tog) twice, m1, k2 tog.
Row 63: s1, k1, psso, k3.
Row 64: m1, (k2 tog) twice.
Row 65: s1, k1, psso, k1.
Row 66: k2 tog.
Cast off.

Work another 3 pieces.
Join and sew to cloth.

NAPKIN LACE

Special abbreviation
inc in this pattern = k into b&f of st

Cast on 2 sts.
Row 1: m1, k2.
Row 2: m1, k2 tog, inc in last st.
Row 3: k4.
Row 4: m1, k2 tog, k1, m1, inc in last st.
Row 5: k6.
Row 6: m1, k2 tog, k1, m1, k2 tog, m1, inc in last st.
Row 7: k8.
Row 8: m1, k2 tog, k1, (m1, k2 tog) twice, m1, inc in last st.

Row 9: k10.
Row 10: m1, k2 tog, k1, (m1, k2 tog) 3 times, m1, inc in last st.
Row 11: k12.
Row 12: m1, k2 tog, k1, (m1, k2 tog) 4 times, m1, inc in last st.
Row 13: k14.
Row 14: m1, k2 tog, k1, (m1, k2 tog) 5 times, m1, inc in last st.
Row 15: k16.
Row 16: m1, k2 tog, k1, (m1, k2 tog) 6 times, m1, inc in last st.
Row 17: k18.
Row 18: m1, k2 tog, k15, inc in last st.
Row 19: s1, k1, (m1, k2 tog) 7 times, m1, k3.
Row 20: m1, k2 tog, k18.
Row 21: Knit.
Row 22: m1, (k2 tog) twice, (m1, k2 tog) 7 times, k2.
Row 23: Knit.
Row 24: m1, (k2 tog) twice, (m1, k2 tog) 6 times, k3.
Row 25: s1, k17.
Row 26: m1, (k2 tog) twice, (m1, k2 tog) 5 times, k4.
Row 27: s1, k to end.
Row 28: m1, (k2 tog) twice, (m1, k2 tog) 4 times, k5.
Row 29: sl 1, k to end of row.

Corner of Lancefield Lace table cloth with matching lace-trimmed napkin

Row 30: m1, (k2 tog) twice, (m1, k2 tog) 3 times, k6.
Row 31 and alternate rows until row 51: sl 1, k to end of row.
Row 32: m1, (k2 tog) twice, (m1, k2 tog) twice, k7.
Row 34: m1, (k2 tog) twice, m1, k2 tog, k8.
Row 36: m1, (k2 tog) twice, m1, k9.
Row 38: m1, k2 tog, k1, m1, k2 tog, m1, k8.
Row 40: m1, k2 tog, k1, (m1, k2 tog) twice, m1, k7.
Row 42: m1, k2 tog, k1, (m1, k2 tog) 3 times, m1, k6.
Row 44: m1, k2 tog, k1, (m1, k2 tog) 4 times, m1, k5.
Row 46: m1, k2 tog, k1, (m1, k2 tog) 5 times, m1, k4.
Row 48: m1, k2 tog, k1, (m1, k2 tog) 6 times, m1, k3.
Row 50: m1, k2 tog, k17.
Row 51: s1, k1, (m1, k2 tog) 7 times, m1, k3.
Repeat rows 20–51 for length required.

Begin second corner:
Row 1: m1, k2 tog, k16, k2 tog.
Row 2: sl 1, k1, psso, k17.
Row 3: m1, (k2 tog) twice, (m1, k2 tog) 7 times.
Row 4: s1, k1, psso, k15.

Row 5: m1, (k2 tog) twice, (m1, k2 tog) 6 times.
Row 6: s1, k1, psso, k13.
Row 7: m1, (k2 tog) twice, (m1, k2 tog) 5 times.
Row 8: s1, k1, psso, k11.
Row 9: m1, (k2 tog) twice, (m1, k2 tog) 4 times.
Row 10: s1, k1, psso, k9.
Row 11: m1, (k2 tog) twice, (m1, k2 tog) 3 times.
Row 12: s1, k1, psso, k7.
Row 13: m1, (k2 tog) twice, (m1, k2 tog) twice.
Row 14: s1, k1, psso, k5.
Row 15: m1, (k2 tog) twice, m1, k2 tog.
Row 16: s1, k1, psso, k3.
Row 17: m1, (k2 tog) twice.
Row 18: s1, k1, psso, k1.
Row 19: k2 tog.
Repeat rows 21–51 until length required, then repeat corner rows 1–19.

Work straight lace section until edging is completed. Join the corners and stitch lace to napkin.

26 GRECIAN LACE

A simple white luncheon mat and napkin, edged with a classic lace. Beautifully knitted by Ruth Rintoule.

Materials
1 x 50 g ball DMC 20
Needles 1.75 mm (15)
Luncheon mat and napkin
Sewing thread and needle for attaching lace

Cast on 9 sts.
Row 1: k1, (m1, k2 tog) to end of row.
Row 2 and alternate rows: k1, m1, k to end of row.
Row 3: k2, (m1, k2 tog) to end of row.
Row 5: k3, (m1, k2 tog) to end of row.

Row 7: k4, (m1, k2 tog) to end of row.
Row 9: k5, (m1, k2 tog) to end of row.
Row 11: k6, (m1, k2 tog) to end of row.
Row 13: k7, (m1, k2 tog) to end of row.
Row 15: k8, (m1, k2 tog) to end of row.
Row 16: Cast off 7 sts, k to end of row.
Repeat rows 1–16 until length required, allowing ample fullness at corners.
Cast off.
Sew to mat and napkin with tiny sts, joining lace at ends.

27 PRESERVE COVERS

Four decorative lace covers for your preserves; designs and basic centres from Edna Lomas.
Clockwise from lower left are Watermelon, Tomatoes, Pumpkin Edging and Carrots.

Materials
DMC 20 cotton, small quantity
Needles 2 mm (14)
The metal-lidded jars have been labelled with fruit magnets available from craft suppliers, adding colour to the pantry shelves.

WATERMELON

Cast on 10 sts: 3 sts on each of 2 needles, 4 sts on 3rd needle. Work with 4th needle.

Round 1: Knit.
Round 2: (m1, k1) to end of round.
Round 3 and alternate rounds: Knit.
Round 4: (m1, k2) to end of round.
Round 6: (m1, k3) to end of round.
Round 8: (m1, k4) to end of round.
Round 10: (m1, k5) to end of round.
Round 12: (m1, k6) to end of round.
Round 14: (m1, k7) to end of round.
Round 16: (m1, k8) to end of round.
Round 18: (m1, k1, m1, sl 1, k1, psso, k6) to end of round.
Round 20: (m1, k3, m1, sl 1, k1, psso, k5) to end of round.
Round 22: (m1, k5, m1, sl 1, k1, psso, k4) to end of round.
Round 24: (m1, k7, m1, sl 1, k1, psso, k3) to end of round.
Round 26: (m1, k1, m1, sl 1, k1, psso, k3, k2 tog, m1, k1, m1, sl 1, k1, psso, k2) to end of round.
Round 28: (m1, k3, m1, sl 1, k1, psso, k1, k2 tog, m1, k3, m1, sl 1, k1, psso, k1) to end of round.
Round 30: (m1, k5, m1, sl 1, k2, psso, m1, k5, m1, sl 1, k1, psso) to end of round.
Round 32: (m1, k3, k2 tog, k2, m1, k1, m1, k2, k2 tog, k3, m1, k1) to end of round.
Cast off picot-wise.

TOMATOES

Cast on 9 sts, 3 sts on each of 3 needles. Work with 4th needle.

Rounds 1 and 2: Knit.
Round 3: (m1, k1) to end of round.
Round 4 and alternate rounds: Knit.
Round 5: (m1, k2) to end of round.
Round 7: (m1, k3) to end of round.
Round 9: (m1, k4) to end of round.
Round 11: (m1, k5) to end of round.
Round 13: (m1, k6) to end of round.
Round 15: (m1, k1, m1, sl 1, k1, psso, k4) to end of round.
Round 17: (m1, k3, m1, sl 1, k1, psso, k3) to end of round.
Round 19: (m1, k2, m1, sl 1, k1, psso, k1, m1, sl 1, k1, psso, k2) to end of round.
Round 20: [(m1, k2, (m1, sl 1, k1, psso) twice, k1, m1, sl 1, k1, psso, k1)] to end of round.
Round 23: [(m1, k2, (m1, sl 1, k1, psso) 3 times, k1, m1, sl 1, k1, psso)] to end of round.
Round 25: [(m1, k2, (m1, sl 1, k1, psso) 5 times)] to end of round.
Round 26: Knit (117 sts).
Purl 5 rows.
Cast off thus:
Knit 1st st, *sl 1 st from RH needle onto LH needle. Insert needle into this st. Cast on 2 sts, then cast off 5 sts. Repeat from * until all sts have been cast off.

PUMPKIN EDGING

Special abbreviation
inc 1 = k in f&b of st

Cast on 6 sts.
Row 1 (right side): inc 1, (m1, k1) twice, m1, k2 tog tbl, k1 (9 sts).
Row 2 and alternate rows: sl 1, p to last 2 sts, p2 tog.
Row 3: inc 1, m1, k2 tog, (m1, k1) twice, m1, k2 tog tbl, k1 (11 sts).

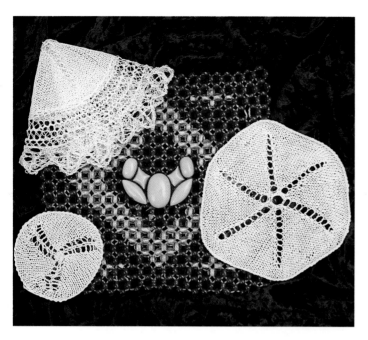

The cover shown folded was made from the coaster pattern on page 86. Edna Lomas supplied the two basic centres—these can be trimmed to your requirements.

Row 5: inc 1, m1, k2 tog, m1, sl2, k1, psso, m1, k1, m1, k2 tog tbl, k1.
Row 7: inc 1, m1, sl2, k1, psso, m1, k3 tog, m1, k2 tog tbl, k1 (9 sts).
Row 9: inc 1, m1, sl2, k2 tog, psso, m1, k2 tog tbl, k1 (7 sts).
Row 10: As row 2 (6 sts).
Repeat rows 1–10 until length required.
Press edging. Sew around centre of preserve cover.

CARROTS EDGING

Cast on 9 sts.
Work foundation row thus: k6, m1, k2 tog, k1.
Row 1: k3, m1, k2 tog, k2, m1, k2 (10 sts).
Row 2: sl 1, k2, m1, k4, m1, k2 tog, k1 (11 sts).
Row 3: k3, m1, k2 tog, m1, k6 (12 sts).
Row 4: Cast off 3 sts, k5, m1, k2 tog, k1 (9 sts).
Repeat rows 1–4 until length required.

BASIC CENTRE A (on left)

Cast on 6 sts: 2 sts on each of 3 needles. Join into circle.
Round 1: (k1, m1) to end of round.
Round 2 and alternate rounds unless otherwise stated: Knit.
Round 3: (k1, m1) to end of round.
Round 5: (k1, m1, k3, m1) to end of round.
Round 7: (k1, m1, k5, m1) to end of round.
Round 9: (k1, m1, k7, m1) to end of round.
Round 11: (k1, m1, k9, m1) to end of round.
Round 13: (k1, m1, k11, m1) to end of round.
Round 15: (k1, m1, k13, m1) to end of round.
Round 17: (k1, m1, k15, m1) to end of round.
Knit 3 rounds.
Cast off.

BASIC CENTRE B (on right)

Cast on 12 sts, 4 sts on each of 3 needles. Join in ring and place marker at join.
Round 1: Knit.
Round 2: *m1, k2, repeat from * to end of round (18 sts).
Round 3 and alternate rounds, unless otherwise stated: Knit, working k1, p1 into each m1 (24 sts).
Round 4: k1 to right, *m1, k4, repeat from * to end of round (30 sts).
Round 6: k1 to right, *m1, k6, repeat from * to end of round (42 sts).
Round 8: k1 to right, *m1, k8, repeat from * to end of round (54 sts).
Round 10: k1 to right, *m1, k10, repeat from * to end of round (66 sts).
Round 12: k1 to right, *m1, k12, repeat from * to end of round (78 sts).
Round 14: k1 to right, *m1, k14, repeat from * to end of round (90 sts).
Round 16: k1 to right, *m1, k16, repeat from * to end of round (102 sts).
Round 18: k1 to right, *m1, k18, repeat from * to end of round (114 sts).
Round 20: k1 to right, *m1, k20, repeat from * to end of round (126 sts).
Rounds 22–27: Knit.
Cast off.

28 LEAF AND TRELLIS LACE

Honeycomb cotton towels and face washer embroidered by Joan Jackson, and trimmed with lace knitted by the author. Suitable for a special gift.

Materials

Towel: DMC 10, needles 2.25 mm (13)
Handtowel: DMC 30, needles 1.25 mm (18)
Facewasher: DMC 10, needles 2 mm (14)
DMC embroidery threads in colours Nos 221, 223, 224, 225, 501, 502, 522.

TOWEL LACE

Cast on 38 sts.
Row 1: m1, k1,m1, k2 tog, m1, k3, (k2 tog) twice, k2, k2 tog, k1, (k2 tog) twice, k1, m1, k2 tog, m1, k5, [m2, (k2 tog) twice] twice, m2, k2 tog, k1.
Row 2 and alternate rows: sl 1, k1, (k and p in next st, k2) twice, k and p in next st, p to end of row.
Row 3: m1, k3, m1, k2 tog, m1, [k2, (k2 tog) twice] twice, m1, k2 tog, m1, k7, [m2, (k2 tog) twice], m2, k2 tog, k1.
Row 5: m1, k5, m1, k2 tog, m1, k1, (k2 tog) twice, k1, (k2 tog, m1) twice, k9, [m2, (k2 tog) twice] twice, m2, k2 tog, k1.

Row 7: m1, k7, (m1, k2 tog) twice, (k2 tog) twice, k2, (k2 tog) twice, k3, m1, k2 tog, m1, k1, [m2, (k2 tog) twice] twice, m2 k2 tog, k1.
Row 9: m1, k9, (m1, k2 tog) twice, k2, (k2 tog) twice, k2, m1, k2 tog, m1, k3, [m2, (k2 tog) twice] twice, m2, k2 tog, k1.
Row 10: As row 2.
Repeat rows 1–10 until length desired.

FACEWASHER

Cast on 8 sts.
Row 1: sl 1, k1, [m1, p2 tog, (k1, p1, k1) in next st] twice.
Row 2: (k3, m1, p2 tog) twice,k2.
Row 3: sl 1, k1, (m1, p2 tog, k3) twice.
Row 4: (cast off 2 sts, m1, p2 tog) twice, k1.
Repeat rows 1–4 until length required.

29 PRIMROSE

Lace handkerchief adapted from a small mat pattern by Ruth Rintoule.

Materials

1 x 50 g ball DMC 40 cotton
Set of 5 double pointed needles 1.75 mm (15)
Finished size 16 cm (6¼″) square

Centre

Cast on 4 sts, one st on each of 4 needles. Work with 5th needle.

Round 1 and alternate rounds: Knit.
Round 2: (m1, k1) to end of round.
Round 4: *(m1, k1) twice, repeat from * to end of round.
Round 6: *m1, k3, m1, k1, repeat from * to end of round.
Round 8: *m1, k5, m1, k1, repeat from * to end of round.
Round 10: *m1, k7, m1, k1, repeat from * to end of round.
Round 12: *(m1, k4, m1, k1) twice, repeat from * to end of round.
Round 14: *m1, k5, m1, k3, m1, k5, m1, k1, repeat from * to end of round.
Round 16: *m1, k6, m1, k5, m1, k6, m1, k1, repeat from * to end of round.
Round 18: *m1, k2 tog, k5, m1, k3, m1, k1, m1, k3, m1, k5, k2 tog, m1, k1. Repeat from * to end of round.
Round 20: *m1, k1, m1, k2 tog, k4, m1, k4, m1, k3, (m1, k4) twice, k2 tog, (m1, k1) twice. Repeat from * to end of round.
Round 22: *m1, (k3, m1, k2 tog) 3 times, k1, k2 tog, m1, (k3, k2 tog, m1) twice, k3, m1, k1. Repeat from * to end of round.
Round 24: *m1, k2 tog, k1, k2 tog, (m1, k2 tog, k2) twice, k2 tog, m1, k3 tog, m1, k2 tog, k2, k2 tog, m1, k2, k2 tog, m1, k2 tog, k1, k2 tog, m1, k1. Repeat from * to end of round.
Round 26: *m1, k1, m1, k3 tog, m1, (k1, m1, k2 tog) twice, k1, k2 tog, (m1, k1) 3 times, m1, k2 tog, k1, k2 tog, m1, k1, k2 tog, m1, k1, m1, k3 tog, (m1, k1) twice. Repeat from * to end of round.
Round 28: *m1, k3, m1, k1, m1, k3, (m1, k2 tog) twice, k2 tog, m1, k3, m1, k1, m1, k3, m1, k2 tog, (k2 tog, m1) twice, k3, m1, k1, m1, k3, m1, k1. Repeat from * to end of round.
Round 30: *m1, k2 tog, k1, k2 tog, m1, k1, m1, k2 tog, k1, k2 tog, m1, k2, k2 tog, m1, k1, k3 tog, k3, k3 tog, k1, m1, k2 tog, k2, m1, k2 tog, k1, k2 tog, m1, k1, m1, k2 tog, k1, k2 tog, m1, k1. Repeat from * to end of round.

Round 32: *m1, k1, m1, k3 tog, m1, k3, m1, k3 tog, m1, k1, m1, k2, k2 tog, m1, k3 tog, k1, k3 tog, m1, k2 tog, k2, m1, k1, m1, k3 tog, m1, k3, m1, k3 tog, (m1, k1) twice. Repeat from * to end of round.
Round 34: *m1, k3, m1, k1, m1, k2 tog, k1, k2 tog, m1, k1, m1, k3, m1, k2 tog, k2, m1, k3 tog, m1, k2, k2 tog, m1, k3, m1, k1, m1, k2 tog, k1, k2 tog, m1, k1, m1, k3, m1, k1. Repeat from * to end of round.
Round 36: *m1, k1, (m1, k3 tog, m1, k3) twice, m1, k3 tog, m1, k1, m1, (k2 tog) twice, k1, (k2 tog) twice, m1, k1, m1, k3 tog, (m1, k3, m1, k3 tog) twice, (m1, k1) twice. Repeat from * to end of round.
Round 38: *m1, k3, (m1, k1, m1, k2 tog, k1, k2 tog) twice, m1, k1, m1, k3, m1, k2 tog, k1, k2 tog, m1, k3, (m1, k1, m1, k2 tog, k1, k2 tog) twice, m1, k1, m1, k3, m1, k1. Repeat from * to end of round.
Round 40: *m1, k1, m1, k3 tog, (m1, k3, m1, k3 tog) 3 times, (m1, k1, m1, k3 tog) twice, (m1, k3, m1, k3 tog) 3 times, (m1, k1) twice.
Round 42: Knit.
Round 44: (m1, k2 tog) to end of round.
Round 46: As round 44.
Round 48: Knit.
Cast off loosely. Press lightly.

Edging

Cast on 13 sts.
Row 1: k3, m1, k3, m1, k1, m2, k2 tog, m3, k2 tog, m2, k2 tog.
Row 2: (k2, p1) twice, k3, p8, k2.
Row 3: k2, k2 tog, m1, k3 tog, m1, k2 tog, p10.
Row 4: Cast off 4 sts, p10, k2.
Repeat rows 1–4 until length required.
Stitch around handkerchief, allowing ample fullness at each corner.

30 LOTUS BUD

Another small handkerchief knitted by Ruth Rintoule. Soft and delicate for a bride, or to add softness to the pocket of a cocktail suit.

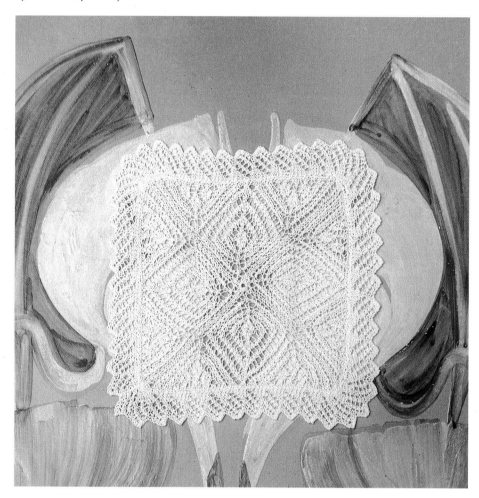

Materials
DMC 100 cotton
Set of 5 double pointed needles 1 mm (20)
Finished size 11.5 cm (4½") square

Square
The following instructions are for one section beginning with 4 sts. Repeat for each of other 3 sections.

Cast on 4 sts on each of 4 needles. Work with 5th needle.
Round 1 and every alternate round: Knit.
Round 2: (m1, k1) 4 times.
Round 4: (k1, m1, k1) 4 times.
Round 6: (k1, m1, k1, m1, k1) 4 times.
Round 8: (k1, m1, k3, m1, k1) 4 times.

Round 10: k1, m1, k2 tog, m1, k1, m1, k2 tog, m1, k1.
Round 12: k1, m1, k2 tog, k1, (m1, k1) twice, k2 tog, m1, k1.
Round 14: k1, m1, k2 tog, k1, m1, k3, m1, k1, k2 tog, m1, k1.
Round 16: k1, m1, k2 tog, k1, m1, k2, m1, k1, m1, k2, m1, k1, k2 tog, m1, k1.
Round 18: (k1, m1, k2 tog) twice, k1, m1, k3, (m1, k1, k2 tog) twice, m1, k1.
Round 20: (k1, m1, k2 tog) twice, k1, m1, k2, m1, k1, m1, k2, (m1, k1, k2 tog) twice, m1, k1.
Round 22: (k1, m1, k2 tog) 3 times, k1, m1, k3, m1, k1, (k2 tog, m1, k1) 3 times.
Round 24: (k1, m1, k2 tog) 3 times, k1, m1, k2, p1, k2, m1, k1, (k2 tog, m1, k1) 3 times.
Round 26: (k1, m1, k2 tog) 3 times, k1, m1, k1, k2 tog,

p1, k2 tog, k1, m1, k1, (k2 tog, m1, k1) 3 times.

Round 28: k1, m1, (k1, m1, k2 tog) 4 times, p1, k2 tog, m1, k1, (k2 tog, m1, k1) 3 times, m1, k1.

Round 30: k1, m1, k2, (k1, m1, k2 tog) 3 times, k1, m1, k3 tog, (m1, k1, k2 tog) 3 times, m1, k3, m1, k1.

Round 32: k1, m1, k2 tog, m1, k1, (m1, k2 tog) twice, k1, m1, k2 tog, k1, m1, k2 tog, k1, (m1, k1) twice, k2 tog, (m1, k1, k2 tog) twice, (m1, k2 tog, m1, k1) twice.

Round 34: k1, m1, k2 tog, k1, m1, k1, m1, k1, k2 tog, m1, k2 tog, (k1, m1, k2 tog) twice, k3, k2 tog, (m1, k1, k2 tog) twice, m1, k2 tog, k1, (m1, k1) twice k2 tog, m1, k1.

Round 36: k1, m1, k2 tog, k1, m1, k3, m1, k1, k2 tog, m1, k2 tog, (k1, m1, k2 tog) twice k1, k2 tog, (m1, k1, k2 tog) twice, m1, k2 tog, k1, m1, k3, m1, k1, k2 tog, m1, k1.

Round 38: k1, m1, k2 tog, k1, m1, k2, m1, k1, m1, k2, m1, k1, k2 tog, m1, k2 tog, k1, m1, k2 tog, k1, m1, k3 tog, (m1, k1, k2 tog) twice, m1, k2 tog, k1, m1, k2, m1, k1, m1, k2, m1, k1, k2 tog, m1, k1.

Round 40: k1, m1, k2 tog, k1, m1, k2 tog, k1, m1, k3, (m1, k1, k2 tog) twice, (m1, k2 tog, k1) twice, (m1, k1) twice, k2 tog, m1, k1, k2 tog, (m1, k2 tog, k1) twice, m1, k3, (m1, k1, k2 tog) twice, m1, k1.

Round 42: (k1, m1, k2 tog) twice, k1, m1, k2, p1, k2, (m1, k1, k2 tog) twice, m1, k2 tog, k1, m1, k2 tog, k3, k2 tog, m1, k1, k2 tog, (m1, k2 tog, k1) twice, m1, k2, p1, k2, (m1, k1, k2 tog) twice, m1, k1.

Round 44: (k1, m1, k2 tog) twice, k1, m1, k1, m1 k2 tog, p1, k2 tog, (m1, k1) twice k2 tog, m1, k1, k2 tog, m1, k2 tog, k1, m1, k2 tog, k1, k2 tog, m1, k1, k2 tog, (m1, k2 tog, k1) twice, m1, k1, m1, k2 tog, p1, k2 tog, (m1, k1) twice, k2 tog, m1, k1, k2 tog, m1, k1.

Round 46: (k1, m1, k2 tog) twice, k1, m1, k3, m1, k3 tog, m1, k3, (m1, k1, k2 tog) twice, m1, k2 tog, k1, m1, k3 tog, m1, k1, k2 tog, m1, k2 tog, k1, m1, k2 tog, k1, m1,

k3, m1, k3 tog, m1, k3, (m1, k1, k2 tog) twice, m1, k1.

Round 48: (k1, m1, k2 tog) 3 times, p1, k2 tog, m1, k1, m1, k2 tog, p1, k2 tog, (m1, k1, k2 tog) twice, m1, k2 tog, k3, k2 tog, m1, k2 tog, (k1, m1, k2 tog) twice, p1, k2 tog, m1, k1, m1, k2 tog, p1, k2 tog, (m1, k1, k2 tog) twice, m1, k1.

Round 50: (k1, m1, k2 tog) 3 times, p1, k2 tog, m1, k1, m1, k2 tog, p1, (k2 tog, m1, k1) twice, k2 tog, m1, k2 tog, k1, k2 tog, m1, k2 tog, (k1, m1, k2 tog) twice, p1, k2 tog, m1, k1, m1, k2 tog, p1, k2 tog, (m1, k1, k2 tog) twice, m1, k1.

Round 52: (k1, m1, k2 tog) twice, k1, m1, k1, m1, k3 tog, m1, k3, m1, k3 tog, (m1, k1) twice, k2 tog, m1, k1, k2 tog, m1, k3 tog, (m1, k2 tog, k1) twice, m1, k1, m1, k3 tog, m1, k3, m1, k3 tog, m1, k1, (m1, k1, k2 tog) twice, m1, k1.

Round 53: Knit.

Cast off.

Edging

Cast on 8 sts.

Knit 1 row.

Row 1: sl 1, (m1, k2 tog) twice, m1, k2.

Row 2 and alternate rows: sl 1, k to end.

Row 3: m1, k2, (m1, k2 tog) twice, m1, k2.

Row 5: m1, k3, (m1, k2 tog) twice, m1, k2.

Row 7: m1, k4, (m1, k2 tog) twice, m1, k2.

Row 9: sl 1, k11.

Row 10: Cast off 4 sts, k to end of row.

Repeat rows 1-10 until length required, allowing ample fullness at corners.

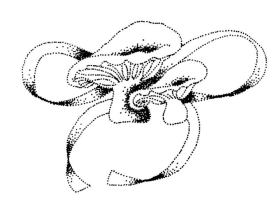

31 NICHOLAS SPRUCE

A Christmas bear designed and knitted by Thea Moore, who also designed and knitted the Christmas sack, stocking, tree skirt, and a beautiful holly leaf. The bear's joints are internal, and his features are embroidered for safety. Thea knitted his muzzle and pads in chenille for contrasting texture.

NICHOLAS SPRUCE

Materials
5 x 50 g balls 12-ply mohair yarn
1 x 50 g ball chenille for muzzle and pads
Pair 3 mm (11) needles
Washable fibre filling and thread for assembling bear
Ribbon for bow if desired

Head

Special abbreviation
inc = k in f&b of st)

Begin at neck.
Cast on 30 sts.
Row 1: Knit.
Row 2 and alternate rows: Purl.
Row 3: Knit.
Row 5: k14, inc in next 2 sts, k14.
Row 7: k15, inc in next 2 sts, k15.
Row 9: k16, inc in next 2 sts, k16.
Row 11: k17, inc in next 2 sts, k17.
Row 13: k17, inc in next 4 sts, k17.
Row 15: k17, inc in next 8 sts, k17.
Row 17: k17, inc in next st, k14, inc in next st, k17.
Row 19: k17, inc in next st, k16, inc in next st, k17.
Row 21: k17, inc in next st, k18, inc in next st, k17.
Row 23: k17, inc in next st, k20, inc in next st, k17.
Row 25: k17, inc in next st, k22, inc in next st, k17.
Row 27: Knit.
Row 29: k17, sl 1, k1, psso, k22, sl 1, k1, psso, k17.
Row 31: k17, sl 1, k1, psso, k20, sl 1, k1, psso, k17.
Row 33: k17, sl 1, k1, psso, k18, sl 1, k1, psso, k17.
Row 35: k17, sl 1, k1, psso, k16, sl 1, k1, psso, k17.
Row 37: k17, sl 1, k1, psso, k14, sl 1, k1, psso, k17.
Row 39: k17, (sl 1, k1, psso) 8 times, k17.
Rows 41–45: st, st.
Row 46: Work in st, st. Dec at beginning of each row until 22 sts remain.
Cast off.
NB: If you are using a different yarn for the bear's muzzle and soles, knit the 17 sts at each end of the needle in main thread, and the central sts in rows 17-39 in contrast.

Back of head
Begin at neck.
Cast on 30 sts.
Row 1: Knit.
Row 2 and alternate rows: Purl.
Row 3: Knit.
Row 5: k14, inc in next 2 sts, k14.
Row 7: k15, inc in next 2 sts, k15.
Row 9: k16, inc in next 2 sts, k16.
Row 11: k17, inc in next 2 sts, k17.
Row 13: k2, inc in next st, k32, inc in next st, k2 (40 sts).
Rows 15–29: Continue, inc as above until there are 50 sts on needle.
Rows 30–45: st, st.
Row 46: k2 tog, k46, k2 tog.
Continue in st, st. Dec at each end of the row until 22 sts remain.
Cast off.

Body

Work in one piece. Begin at neck edge.
Cast on 60 sts.
Row 1: Knit.
Row 2 and alternate rows: Purl.
Row 3: k16, inc in next 2 sts, k24, inc in next 2 sts, k16.
Row 5: k17, inc in next 2 sts, k26, inc in next 2 sts, k17.
Row 7: k18, inc in next 2 sts, k28, inc in next 2 sts, k18.
Row 9: k19, inc in next 2 sts, k30, inc in next 2 sts, k19.
Row 11: k20, inc in next 2 sts, k32, inc in next 2 sts, k20.
Row 13: k21, inc in next 2 sts, k34, inc in next 2 sts, k21.
Row 15: k22, inc in next 2 sts, k36, inc in next 2 sts, k22.
Row 17: k23, inc in next 2 sts, k38, inc in next 2 sts, k23.
Rows 18–47: St, st.
Row 48: k23, (k2 tog) twice, k38, (k2 tog) twice, k23.
Row 50: k22, (k2 tog) twice, k36, (k2 tog) twice, k22.
Row 52: k21, (k2 tog) twice, k34, (k2 tog) twice, k21.
Row 54: k20, (k2 tog) twice, k32, (k2 tog) twice, k20.
Row 56: k19, (k2 tog) twice, k30, (k2 tog) twice, k19.
Row 58: k18, (k2 tog) twice, k28, (k2 tog) twice, k18.
Row 60: k17, (k2 tog) twice, k26, (k2 tog) twice, k17.

Row 62: k16, (k2 tog) twice, k24, (k2 tog) twice, k16.
Row 64: k15, (k2 tog) twice, k22, (k2 tog) twice, k15.
Row 66: Knit.
Cast off.

Legs

Begin at sole.
Cast on 20 sts.
Row 1: Knit.
Row 2 and alternate rows: Purl.
Row 3: Knit, inc in each st.
Row 5: Knit, inc in alternate sts.
Row 7: Knit.
Row 9: Knit, inc in every 4th st.
Rows 10–18: st, st.
Change to contrasting thread if desired.
Row 19: k20, (k2 tog) 18 times, k19.
Row 20: k20, (k2 tog) 9 times, k19.
Rows 21–73: st, st.
Row 74: k2 tog, k22, k2 tog, k20, k2 tog.
Row 76: k2 tog, k20, k2 tog, k19, k2 tog.
Row 78: k2 tog, k18, k2 tog, k18, k2 tog.
Row 80: k2 tog, k17, k2 tog, k16, k2 tog.
Row 82: k2 tog, k15, k2 tog, k15, k2 tog.
Row 84: (k2 tog) twice, k11, (k2 tog) twice, k10, (k2 tog) twice.
Row 86: (k2 tog), twice, k8, (k2 tog) twice, k7, (k2 tog) twice.
Row 88: (k2 tog) 10 times, k1.
Row 89: Purl.
Cast off.

Ears (make 2)

Begin with bottom of ear.
Cast on 10 sts.
Row 1: Knit.
Row 2: Purl.
Row 3: k2, inc in 3rd, 5th and 7th sts, k3.
Row 4: Purl.
Row 5: k2, inc in 3rd, 5th, 7th, 9th and 11th, k2.
Rows 6–10: st, st.
Row 11: k2 tog, k16.
Row 12: k2 tog, p15.
Continue, dec in this manner until 9 sts remain.
Cast off.

Arms (make 2)

Begin at top of arm.
Cast on 5 sts.
Row 1: Knit.
Row 2 and alternate rows: Purl.
Rows 3, 5 and 7: Knit inc in each st.

Row 9: k4, inc in the 5th st to end of row.
Rows 10–30: st, st.
Shape lower arm thus:
Row 31: k20, turn, purl back.
Row 32: k15, turn, purl back.
Row 33: k10, turn, purl back.
Row 34: k5, turn, purl back.
Row 35: k4, k2 tog, (k3, k2 tog) 3 times, k2, k2 tog, k27.
Row 36: p20, turn, purl back.
Row 37: p15, turn, purl back.
Row 38: p10, turn, purl back.
Row 39: p5, turn, purl back.
Row 40: p4, p2 tog, (p3, p2 tog) 3 times, p2, p2 tog, p18.
Rows 41–56: st, st.
Row 57: k2 tog, (k16, k2 tog) twice.
Row 58: Purl.
Row 59: k2 tog, k14, k2 tog, k15, k2 tog.
Row 60: Purl.
Row 61: k2 tog, (k13, k2 tog) twice.
Row 62: Purl.
Row 63: k2 tog, k11, k2 tog, k12, k2 tog.
Row 64: Purl.
Row 65: k2 tog, (k10, k2 tog) twice.
Row 66: Purl.
Row 67: k2 tog, k8, k2 tog, k9, k2 tog.
Row 68: Purl.
Cast off.

To make up bear
Sew seams of arms and legs, leaving top open to allow placing of joints or firmly secured buttons, which are attached before the body is filled. Close tops of arms and legs. The bottom of the body is the last seam to be closed. The neck joint is put into place after the eyes, nose are attached and the filling is put into the head. The neck joint is secured by the gathering of the neck part of the head after sewing the head. The ears are sewn in place in the head seam. Trim the bear's neck with a large bow or collar.

CHRISTMAS STOCKING

Materials
DMC 20 cotton
Needles 1 mm (20)
Small quantity mohair for stocking top

Special abbreviation
inc = k in f&b of the st

Cast on 80 sts.
Row 1: Knit.
Row 2: Purl.

Row 3: k1, inc in next st, k37, inc in next 2 sts, k37, inc in next st, k1.
Row 4: Purl.
Rows 5–13: Repeat rows 3–4, inc as before (104 sts).
Rows 14–22: st, st.
Row 23: k 51, k2 tog, k to end of row.
Row 24: Purl.
Rows 25–30: Repeat rows 23–24. Dec in centre 2 sts on k row (100 sts).
Row 31: k to centre 4 sts, (k2 tog) twice, turn, (p2 tog) twice, turn. Continue shaping foot until 30 sts remain at each end. Knit to end of row.
Rows 32–72: st, st.
Knit 10 rows in contrasting thread for stocking top.

HOLLY LEAF

Materials
Small quantity green cotton
Needles 1.25 mm (18)

Cast on 3 sts.
Row 1: Knit.
Row 2: Purl.
Row 3: k1, k in f&b of next st, k1.
Row 4: Purl.
Row 5: (k1, m1) to last st, k1.
Row 6: Purl.
Rows 7–10: Repeat rows 5–6 until there are 25 sts on needle.
Row 11: Cast off 5 sts, k to end of row.
Row 12: Cast off 5 sts, p to end of row.
Row 13: (k3, m1) to last 3 sts, k3.
Row 14: Purl.
Row 15: (k5, m1) to last 4 sts, k4.
Row 16: Purl.
Repeat rows 11–16 twice.
Row 23: Cast off 1 st at beginning of each row until 2 sts remain.
Cast off.
Press the leaf under a damp cloth. Attach to the Christmas stocking.

CHRISTMAS SACK

Materials
1 x 50 g ball DMC Hermina, ecru

Cast on 52 sts, or multiples of 4 sts if a smaller or larger size sack is desired.

Row 1: Knit.
Row 2: [(k4, turn, p4) twice)] k4. Repeat to end of row.
Row 3: Purl.
Repeat rows 2–3 until length required.
Cast off.
Sew side seams, insert knitted cord (see pattern for Christmas Tree Skirt) or ribbon through holes after first row 3 to draw the sack closed.
For oval base of the sack, shape thus:
After working first side of sack proceed as follows:
Row 1: k to last 4 sts. Turn, p to end. Repeat 12 times, inc by 4 sts before each turn.
Row 2: k4, turn, purl to end. Repeat 12 times, inc by 4 sts before each turn.
The shaped base enables the sack to stand upright.

CHRISTMAS TREE SKIRT

Materials
2 x 50 g balls 4-ply cotton
Needles 2 mm (14)

Cast on 75 sts.
Row 1: Knit.
Row 2: Purl.
Row 3: k1, m1, k to last 5 sts, turn, purl back.
Row 4: Repeat row 3 increasing by 5 sts before each turn, purl back.
Row 5: k1, (m1, k2 tog, k3) until last 5 sts, m1, k5.
Row 6: Purl.
Row 7: k1, m1, (k2 tog) twice, k to last 5 sts, turn, purl back.
Row 8: Repeat row 7, dec as before until last 5 sts. k5.
Repeat rows 3–7 to form circle.
Cast off.
To enlarge circle, inc by multiples of 5.
Skirt can be fastened by ribbon bows, or the seam sewn.
The circle can be used as a small table cover.
To make the points of the skirt more definite, edge with knitted cord. Decorate as desired.

Work knitted cord thus:
Using double pointed needles, cast on 3 sts, *k3. Do not turn. Slide sts to other end of needle, pull yarn firmly*.
Repeat *–* until length required.

32 ICE CRYSTAL FAIRY

A Christmas fairy designed by Thea Moore. Thea's designs for the wings and dress are most unusual and effective. Each ribbon is secured by a colonial knot, for which instructions are included.

Materials
18 cm (7″) doll
2 x 20 g balls DMC 20
Needles 1.25 mm (18)
Net for underskirt if desired
1 m (40″) silver ribbon
Adhesive dots to secure wings
Needle and thread for working colonial knots to attach ribbons

Dress

Cast on 76 sts.
Row 1: Knit.
Row 2: Purl.
Row 3: k1, m1, k to last 10 sts, turn, purl back (this forms bodice).
Row 4: Repeat row 3, increasing by 5 sts before each turn.
Row 5: Purl.
Row 6: k1, m1, k2 tog, k7, (m1, k2 tog, k3) until last 10 sts, k10.
Row 7: Purl.
Row 8: k1, m1, (k2 tog) twice, k to last 10 sts, turn, purl back.
Row 9: k1, m1, (k2 tog) twice, k to last 15 sts, turn, purl back.
Row 10: Repeat row 9, increasing by 5 sts before each turn.
Repeat rows 1–10, 11 times.
Cast off and press.
Sew back seam. Thread silver ribbon through the holes in the centre of each panel. If the ribbon is looped around for the rows either side of the centre, it will hold the dress on the doll's shoulders.

Wings

Cast on 20 sts.
Row 1: Knit.
Row 2 and alternate rows: Purl.
Rows 3, 5, 7, 9, 11, 13 and 15: k1, m1, k to last st, m1, k1.
Row 17: k1, m1, (k2, m1) 16 times, k1.
Row 19: k1, m1, (k3, m1) 16 times, k1, m1, k1.
Row 21: k1, m1, (k4, m1) 16 times, k6, m1, k1.
Row 23: k1, m1, (k5, m1) 16 times, k8, m1, k1.
Row 25: k1, m1, (k6, m1) 16 times, k10, m1, k1.
Row 27: k1, m1, (k7, m1) 16 times, k12, m1, k1.
Row 29: k1, m1, (k8, m1) 16 times, k14, m1, k1.
Row 31: k1, m1, (k9, m1) 16 times, k16, m1, k1.
Row 33: k1, m1, k2 tog, k8, m1, (k2 tog, k8, m1) 15 times, k14, k2 tog, m1, k1.
Row 34: Purl.

Repeat rows 33–34, 5 times.
Row 43: k1, m1, k2 tog, k8, m1, (k2 tog, k8, m1) 15 times, k12, turn, purl back.
Row 44: k1, m1, k2 tog, k8, m1, (k2 tog, k8, m1) 13 times, k10, turn, purl back.
Row 45: k1, m1, k2 tog, k8, m1, (k2 tog, k8, m1) 11 times, k8, turn, purl back.
Row 46: k1, m1, k2 tog, k8, m1, (k2 tog, k8, m1) 9 times, k6, turn, purl back.
Row 47: k1, m1, k2 tog, k8, m1, (k2 tog, k8, m1) 7 times, k4, turn, purl back.
Row 48: k1, m1, k2 tog, k8, m1, (k2 tog, k8, m1) 5 times, k2, turn, purl back.
Row 49: k1, m1, k2 tog, k8, m1, (k2 tog, k8, m1) 3 times, turn, purl back.
Row 50: k1, m1, k2 tog, k8, m1, (k2 tog, k8, m1) once, turn, purl back.
Row 51: (k2 tog, m1, k2 tog) to end of row.
Row 52: Purl.
Cast off.

To make an exact mirror image for the other wing, change the order of the knit and purl rows, i.e. *Row 1:* Purl, *Row 2:* Knit. The knit row becomes the alternate row.

To form wing flutes
Crochet the wing segments into flutes by joining thread to the tip of the top of the wing. Work 3ch, sc into next segment. Crochet until all segments have been joined. Do not join bottom tip—this should hang with a bead attached.

The wings can be attached to the doll with adhesive dots, or sewn into position.

Colonial knot

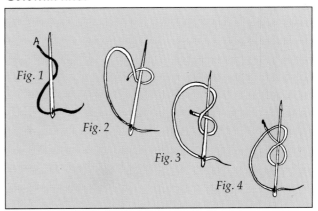

Bring needle up at A. Hold thread toward you and point needle away from you. Place needle over thread and pick up to form a loop (figs 1 and 2). Take thread over needle (fig. 3) to form a figure eight (fig. 4). Insert needle back into fabric at A. Roll knot down needle firmly and pull through to form colonial knot.

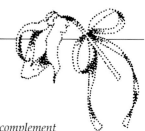

33 BOTTLE CARDIGAN

An interesting pattern from the past. Barbara Hosking adapted this pattern and made the coaster to complement the cardigan. The cover is practical too!

KNITTED CARDIGAN, OR BOTTLE COVER.

This article forms a most useful and acceptable present to friends in the East and West Indies, where wine, instead of being decanted, is brought to table in the black bottle, the ugliness of which is rather heightened than disguised by a common calico covering.

As an improvement, I have introduced the cardigan, or bottle cover, which looks very pretty, and serves the purpose of keeping the bottle cool. Some are done in crochet, but the knitted ones, being more close and solid, are preferable.

From *The Home Circle: Accomplishments for Ladies* by Aiguillette.

Materials
1 x 50 g ball DMC 10
Needles 2 mm (14)
Enlarged, this pattern would be suitable for a lamp base.

BOTTLE CARDIGAN

Cast on 36 sts on each of 2 needles, and 24 sts on 3rd needle. Working with 4th needle, join into circle and place marker at join.
Knit one round.
Work 26 rows in p2, k2, rib.
Commence leaf pattern thus:
Round 1: (p4, k1, k2 tog, k6, p2, m1, k1, m1) 6 times.
Round 2: (p4, k1, k2 tog, k5, p2, k3) 6 times.
Round 3: [(p4, k1, k2 tog, k4, p2, k1, (m1, k1) twice)] 6 times.
Round 4: (p4, k1, k2 tog, k3, p2, k5) 6 times.
Round 5: (p4, k1, k2 tog, k2, p2, k2, m1, k1, m1, k2) 6 times.
Round 6: (p4, k1, k2 tog, k1, p2, k7) 6 times.
Round 7: (p4, k1, k2 tog, p2, k3, m1, k1, m1, k3) 6 times.
Round 8: (p4, k2 tog, p2, k9) 6 times.
Round 9: (p4, m1, k1, m1, p2, k1, k2 tog, k6) 6 times.
Round 10: (p4, k3, p2, k1, k2 tog, k5) 6 times.
Round 11: [(p4, k1, (m1, k1) twice, p2, k1, k2 tog, k4)] 6 times.
Round 12: (p4, k5, p2, k1, k2 tog, k3) 6 times.
Round 13: (p4, k2, m1, k1, m1, k2, p2, k1, k2 tog, k2) 6 times.
Round 14: (p4, k7, p2, k1, k2 tog, k1) 6 times.
Round 15: (p4, k3, m1, k1, m1, k3, p2, k1, k2 tog) 6 times.
Round 16: (p4, k9, p2, k2 tog) 6 times.
Repeat rounds 1–16 until cover reaches the slope of the neck.

Shaping the top of bottle cover:
Round 1: (p1, p2 tog, p1, k1, k2 tog, k6, p2, m1, k1, m1) 6 times.
Round 2: (p3, k1, k2 tog, k5, p2, k3) 6 times.
Round 3: [(p1, p2 tog, k1, k2 tog, k4, p2, k1, (m1, k1) twice)] 6 times.
Round 4: (p2, k1, k2 tog, k3, p2, k5) 6 times.

Round 5: [(p2, k1, (k2 tog) twice, p2, k2, m1, k1, m1, k2)] 6 times.
Round 6: (p2, k3 tog, p2, k7) 6 times.
Round 7: (p2, m1, k1, m1, p2, k1, k2 tog, k2, k2 tog) 6 times.
Round 8: (p2, k3, p2, k1, k2 tog, k2) 6 times.
Round 9: [(p2, k1, (m1, k1) twice, p2, k1, k3 tog)] 6 times.
Round 10: (p2, k5, p2, k2 tog) 6 times.

85

Round 11: (p2, k2 tog, m1, k1, m1, k2 tog, p2, k1) 6 times.
Round 12: (p2, k2 tog, k3, p2, k2 tog) 6 times.
Round 13: (p2, k2 tog, k2, p2, k1) 6 times.
Round 14: (p2, k2 tog, k1, p2, k1) 6 times.
Round 15: (p2, k2 tog, p2, k1) 6 times.
Round 16: (p2, k1) to end of round.
Repeat round 16, 28 times.
Cast off ribwise.

BOTTLE COASTER

Cast on 15 sts.
Row 1: sl 1, k1, (m1, k2 tog) 4 times, (m2, k2 tog) twice, k1.
Row 2: k3, p1, k2, p1, k1, (m1, k2 tog) 4 times, k1.
Row 3: sl 1, k1, (m1, k2 tog) 4 times, k2, (m2, k2 tog) twice, k1.
Row 4: k3, p1, k2, p1, k3, (m1, k2 tog) 4 times, k1.
Row 5: sl 1, k1, (m1, k2 tog) 4 times, k4, (m2, k2 tog) twice, k1.
Row 6: k3, p1, k2, p1, k5, (m1, k2 tog) 4 times, k1.

Row 7: sl 1, k1, (m1, k2 tog) 4 times, k6, (m2, k2 tog) twice, k1.
Row 8: k3, p1, k2, p1, k7, (m1, k2 tog) 4 times, k1.
Row 9: sl 1, k1, (m1, k2 tog) 4 times, k13.
Row 10: Cast off 8 sts, k5, (m1, k2 tog) 4 times, k1.
Repeat rows 1–10, 14 times.
Cast off.
Sew seam to form circle.

Using set of double pointed needles, pick up and knit 31 sts on each of 2 needles and 29 sts on 3rd needle (91 sts).
Knit 3 rounds.
Round 4: (k11, k2 tog) to end of round.
Round 5: Knit.
Round 6: (k10, k2 tog) to end of round.
Continue dec in this manner until you have worked (k7, k2 tog).
Dec every round for 7 rounds.
Cut yarn and thread through remaining sts. Fasten off.
Slightly stiffen work to form coaster for bottle

34 NANDINA COLLECTION

Materials
4-ply DMC Hermina (the thicker thread is absorbent)
Needles 2 mm (14)

FILIGREE LACE PLATE

Cast on 8 sts: 3 sts on each of 2 needles, 2 sts on 3rd needle. Work with 4th needle.
Round 1: Knit.
Round 2: (m1, k1) to end of round (16 sts).
Knit 3 rounds.
Round 6: As round 2 (32 sts).
Knit 3 rounds.
Round 10: k1, (m1, k2) to last st, m1, k1 (48 sts).
Round 11: k1, (k1, p1 in m1 of previous round, k2), repeat to last 2 sts, k1, p1 in m1 of previous round,k1 (64 sts).
Round 12: (k2 tog, m1, sl 1, k1, psso) to end of round (48 sts).
Repeat rounds 11 and 12, 4 times.
Round 21: k1, (k1, p1, k1 into m1 of previous round, k2).
Repeat to last 2 sts, k1, p1, k1 into m1 of previous round, k1 (80 sts).
Knit 3 rounds.
Round 25: (m1, k5) to end of round (96 sts).
Round 26 and alternate rounds: Knit.
Round 27: (inc in next st, m1, sl 1, k1, psso, k1, k2 tog, m1). repeat to end of round. Knit 1st st of round onto end of last needle (thus moving end of round). This will now be referred to as k 1st st (112 sts).
Round 29: k2, (m1, sl 1, k2 tog, psso, m1, k4), repeat to end of round, ending last repeat with k2 instead of k4.
Round 31: (m1, k7), repeat to end of round (128 sts).
Round 33: (inc in next st, m1, sl 1, k1, psso, k3, k2 tog, m1), repeat to end of round, k 1st st (144 sts).
Round 35: k2, (m1, sl 1, k1, psso, k1, k2 tog, m1, k4), repeat to end of round, ending last repeat with k2 instead of k4.
Round 37: (m1, k3, m1, sl 1, k2 tog, psso, m1, k3), repeat to end of round (160 sts).
Round 39: (k1, m1, sl 1, k1, psso, k5, k2 tog, m1), repeat to end of round.
Round 41: (m1, k2 tog, m1, sl 1, k1, psso, k3, k2 tog, m1, k1), repeat to end of round.
Round 43: (sl 1, k1, psso, m1, k1, m1, sl 1, k1, psso, k1, k2 tog, m1, sl 1, k1, psso, m1), repeat to end of round.

Round 45: [(m1, k2 tog) twice, m1, sl 1, k2 tog, psso, m1, k1, m1, k2 tog], repeat to end of round.
Round 47: (sl 1, k1, psso, m1), repeat to end of round.
Round 48: Knit.
Round 49: (m1, k2 tog), repeat to end of round.
Round 50: Knit.
Insert needle into next st, cast on 8 sts for lace edging.
Row 1: k8, turn.
Row 2: sl 1, k2, m1, k2 tog, m2, k2 tog, k1.
Row 3: k3, p1, k2, m1, (k2 tog) twice, (last k2 tog uses one st of edging and one st of centre), turn.
Row 4: sl 1, k2, m1, k2 tog, k1, m2, k2 tog, k1.
Row 5: k3, p1, k3, m1, (k2 tog) twice, turn.
Row 6: sl 1, k2, m1, k2 tog, k2, m2, k2 tog, k1.
Row 7: k3, p1, k4, m1, (k2 tog) twice, turn.
Row 8: sl 1, k2, m1, k2 tog, k6.
Row 9: Cast off 3 sts, k5, m1, (k2 tog) twice, turn.
Repeat rows 2–9 until all centre sts have been worked.
Cast off.
Join ends of edging. Press lightly. Stiffen as desired.

GRIGLANS DOILY

Cast on 31 sts.
Row 1: sl 1, k14, (m1, k2 tog) twice, k7, (m2, k2 tog) twice, k1.
Row 2: k3, p1, k2, p1, k24. Turn 2 sts left on needle.
Row 3: sl 1, k13, (m1, k2 tog) twice, k8, (m2, k2 tog) twice, k1.
Row 4: k3, p1, k2, p1, k24. Turn 4 sts left on needle.
Row 5: sl 1, k12, (m1, k2 tog) twice, k9, (m2, k2 tog) twice, k1.
Row 6: k3, p1, k2, p1, k24. Turn 6 sts left on needle.
Row 7: sl 1. k11, (m1, k2 tog) twice, k10, (m2, k2 tog) twice, k1.
Row 8: k3, p1, k2, p1, k24. Turn 8 sts left on needle.
Row 9: sl 1, k10, (m1, k2 tog) twice, k16.
Row 10: Cast off 8 sts, k20. Turn 10 sts left on needle.
Row 11: sl 1, k9, (m1, k2 tog) twice, k2, (m2, k2 tog) twice, k1.
Row 12: k3, p1, k2, p1, k14. Turn 12 sts left on needle.
Row 13: sl 1, k8, (m1, k2 tog) twice, k3, (m2, k2 tog) twice, k1.
Row 14: k3,p1, k2, p1, k14. Turn 14 sts left on needle.
Row 15: sl 1, k7, (m1, k2 tog) twice, k4, (m2, k2 tog) twice, k1.
Row 16: k3, p1, k2, p1, k14. Turn 16 sts left on needle.

Row 17: sl 1, k6, (m1, k2 tog) twice, k5, (m2, k2 tog) twice, k1.

Row 18: k3, p1, k2, p1, k14. Turn 18 sts left on needle.

Row 19: sl 1, k5, (m1, k2 tog) twice, k11.

Row 20: Cast off 8 sts, k30.

Rerp)eat rows 1–20 until you have worked 14 sections, to form circle.

Cast off.

Fasten off thread at the centre, and carefully join side seam.

WELSH WELT

Cast on 26 sts.

Knit 1 row.

Row 1: sl 1, k2, m1, k2 tog, k1, m1, k2 tog, k12, (m1, k2 tog) 3 times.

Row 2: m1, k6, p12, k1, m1, k2 tog, k2, m1, k2 tog, k1 tbl.

Row 3: sl 1, k2, (m1, k2 tog, k1) twice, (m1, k2 tog) 5 times, k1, m1, k2 tog, k1, (m1, k2 tog) twice.

Row 4: m1, k7, p12, k1, m1, k2 tog, k2, m1, k2 tog, k1 tbl.

Row 5: sl 1, k2, (m1, k2 tog, k1) twice, m1, k2 tog, k6, m1, k2 tog, k1, m1, k2 tog, k2, (m1, k2 tog) twice.

Row 6: m1, k8, p12, k1, m1, k2 tog, k2, m1, k2 tog, k1 tbl.

Row 7: sl 1, k2, (m1, k2 tog, k1) twice, (m1, k2 tog) 5 times, k1, m1, k2 tog, k3, (m1, k2 tog) twice.

Row 8: m1, k9, p12, k1, m1, k2 tog, k2, m1, k2 tog, k1 tbl.

Row 9: sl 1, k2, m1, k2 tog, k1, m1, k2 tog, k12, m1, k2 tog, k4, (m1, k2 tog) twice.

Row 10: m1, k23, m1, k2 tog, k2, m1, k2 tog, k1 tbl.

Row 11: sl 1, k2, m1, k2 tog, k1, m1, k2 tog, p12, m1, k2 tog, k5, (m1, k2 tog) twice.

Row 12: m1, k24, m1, k2 tog, k2, m1, k2 tog, k1 tbl.

Row 13: sl 1, k2, m1, k2 tog, k1, m1, k2 tog, p12, m1, k2 tog, k6, (m1, k2 tog) twice.

Row 14: Cast off 6 sts, k18, m1, k2 tog, k2, m1, k2 tog, k1 tbl.

Repeat rows 1–14 until length required.

BOUTIQUE LACE

Cast on 30 sts.

Row 1: sl 1, k1, (m1, p2 tog) twice, k1, k2 tog, m2, (k2 tog) twice, m2, k2 tog, k1, (m1, p2 tog) twice, k2, (m2, k2 tog) twice.

Row 2: k2, (p1, k2) twice, (m1, p2 tog) twice, (k3, p1) 3 times, k2, (m1, p2 tog) twice, k2.

Row 3: sl 1, k1, (m1, p2 tog) twice, k3, k2 tog, m2, (k2 tog) twice, m2, k2 tog, k3, (m1, p2 tog) twice, k8.

Row 4: k8, (m1, p2 tog) twice, k5, p1, k3, p1, k4, (m1, p2 tog) twice, k2.

Row 5: sl 1, k1, (m1, p2 tog) twice, k1, k2 tog, m2, (k2 tog) twice, m2, (k2 tog) twice, m2, k2 tog, k1, (m1, p2 tog) twice, k2, (m2, k2 tog) 3 times.

Row 6: k2, (p1, k2) 3 times, (m1, p2 tog) twice, (k3, p1) 3 times, k2, (m1, p2 tog) twice, k2.

Row 7: sl 1, k1, (m1, p2 tog) twice, k3, k2 tog, m2, (k2 tog) twice, m2, k2 tog, k3, (m1, p2 tog) twice, k11.

Row 8: k11, (m1, p2 tog) twice, k5, p1, k3, p1, k4, (m1, p2 tog) twice, k2.

Row 9: sl 1, k1, (m1, p2 tog) twice, k1, k2 tog, m2, (k2 tog) twice, m2, (k2 tog) twice, m2, k2 tog, k1, (m1, p2 tog) twice, k2, (m2, k2 tog) 4 times, k1.

Row 10: k3, (p1, k2) 4 times, (m1, p2 tog) twice, (k3, p1) 3 times, k2, (m1, p2 tog) twice, k2.

Row 11: sl 1, k1, (m1, p2 tog) twice, k3, k2 tog, m2, (k2 tog) twice, m2, k2 tog, k3, (m1, p2 tog) twice, k15.

Row 12: Cast off 9 sts, k5, (m1, p2 tog) twice, k5, p1, k3, p1, k4, (m1, p2 tog) twice, k2.

Repeat rows 1–12 until length required.

CAKE CIRCLE

Cast on 33 sts.

Row 1: m1, k2 tog, sl 1, k2 tog, psso, (m2, sl 1, k2 tog, psso) 5 times, m2, k2 tog, k1, k2 tog, m2, k2 tog, k3, m1, k2 tog, k1.

Row 2: k8, p1, k4, p1, (k2, p1) 5 times, k2 tog, k1.

Row 3: m1, k2 tog, sl 1, k2 tog, psso, (m2, sl 1, k2 tog, psso) 4 times, m2, k2 tog, k3, k2 tog, m2, k2 tog, k2, m1, k2 tog, k1.

Row 4: k7, p1, k6, p1, (k2, p1) 4 times, k2 tog, k1.

Row 5: m1, k2 tog, sl 1, k2 tog, psso, (m2, sl 1, k2 tog, psso) 3 times, m2, k2 tog, k5, k2 tog, m2, k2 tog, k1, m1, k2 tog, k1.

Row 6: k6, p1, k8, p1, (k2, p1) 3 times, k2 tog, k1.

Row 7: m1, k2 tog, sl 1, k2 tog, psso, (m2, sl 1, k2 tog, psso) twice, m2, k2 tog, k7, k2 tog, m2, k2 tog, m1, k2 tog, k1.

Row 8: k5, p1, k10, p1, (k2, p1) twice, k2 tog, k1.

Row 9: m1, k2 tog, (sl 1, k2 tog, psso, m2) twice, k2 tog, k9, k2 tog, m1, k1, m1, k2 tog, k1.

Row 10: k17, p1, k2, p1, k3.
Row 11: m1, k2, (m2, sl 1, k2 tog, psso) twice, m2, k2 tog, k7, k2 tog, m2, k2 tog, m1, k2 tog, k1.
Row 12: k5, p1, k10, p1, (k2, p1) twice, k3.
Row 13: m1, k2, (m2, sl 1, k2 tog, psso) 3 times, m2, k2 tog, k5, k2 tog, m2, k2 tog, k1, m1, k2 tog, k1.
Row 14: k6, p1, k8, p1, (k2, p1) 3 times, k3.
Row 15: m1, k2, (m2, sl 1, k2 tog, psso) 4 times, m2, k2 tog, k3, k2 tog, m2, k2 tog, k2, m1, k2 tog, k1.

Row 16: k7, p1, k6, p1, (k2, p1) 4 times, k3.
Row 17: m1, k2, (m2, sl 1, k2 tog, psso) 5 times, m2, k2 tog, k1, k2 tog, m2, k2 tog, k3, m1, k2 tog, k1.
Row 18: k8, p1, k4, p1, (k2, p1) 5 times, k3.
Row 19: m1, k2, (m2, sl 1, k2 tog, psso) 7 times, m2, k2 tog, k4, m1, k2 tog, k1.
Row 20: k9, p1, (k2, p1) 7 times, k2 tog, k1.
Repeat rows 1–20 until length required.

35 RETICULE

A knitted bag worked from an 1897 pattern by Ruth Rintoule. The bag was originally designed as a scrap bag; other uses would be as a stocking bag or a lingerie holder, a charming gift for a bride or mother-to-be.

Materials
2 x 50 g balls DMC 10
Set of double pointed needles 2.25 mm (13)
Silk or knitted cord

RETICULE

Cast on 8 sts: 2 sts on 1st needle, 3 sts on each of 2 needles. Work with 4th needle.
Knit 1 round.
Round 1: (m1, k1) to end of round.
Round 2 and alternate rows: Knit.
Round 3: (m1, k2) to end of round.
Round 5: (m1, k3) to end of round.
Round 7: (m1, k4) to end of round.
Round 9: (m1, k5) to end of round.

Round 11: (m1, k6) to end of round.
Round 13: (m1, k7) to end of round.
Round 15: (m1, k8) to end of round.
Round 17: (m1, k9) to end of round.
Round 19: (m1, k10) to end of round.
Round 21: *m1, k1, m1, k2 tog, k8. Repeat from * 7 times.
Round 23: *m1, k1, (m1, k2 tog) twice, k7. Repeat from * 7 times.
Round 25: *m1, k1, (m1, k2 tog) 3 times, k6. Repeat from * 7 times.
Round 27: *m1, k1, (m1, k2 tog) 4 times, k5. Repeat from * 7 times.
Round 29: *m1, k1, (m1, k2 tog) 5 times, k4. Repeat from * 7 times.
Round 31: *m1, k1, (m1, k2 tog) 6 times, k3. Repeat from * 7 times.
Round 33: *m1, k1, (m1, k2 tog) 7 times, k2. Repeat from * 7 times.

Round 35: *m1, k1, (m1, k2 tog) 8 times, k1. Repeat from * 8 times.

Round 37: *m1, k1, (m1, k2 tog) 9 times. Repeat from * 7 times.

Rounds 38, 39, 40 and 41: Knit.

Round 42: *(m1, k2 tog) 7 times, k2. Repeat from * 9 times.

Rounds 43–44: Knit.

Round 45: *m1, k2 tog, k10, m1, k2 tog, k2. Repeat from * 9 times.

Rounds 46–47: Knit.

Round 48: *m1, k2 tog, k2, (m1, k2 tog) 3 times, k2, m1, k2 tog, k2. Repeat from * 9 times

Round 49–50: Knit.

Round 51: *(m1, k2 tog, k2) 4 times. Repeat from * 9 times.

Round 52–53: Knit.

Round 54: *m1, k2 tog, k2, (m1, k2 tog) 3 times, k2, m1, k2 tog, k2. Repeat from * 9 times.

Rounds 55–56: Knit.

Round 57: m1, k2 tog, k10, *m1, k2 tog, k2, m1, k2 tog, k10. Repeat from * 9 times, m1, k2 tog, k2.

Rounds 58–59: Knit.

Round 60: *(m1, k2 tog) 7 times, k2. Repeat from * 9 times.

Rounds 61–64: Knit.

Round 65: (m1, k2 tog) to end of round.

Round 66 and alternate rows: Knit.

Round 67: k1, *(m1, k2 tog) 7 times, k2. Repeat from * 8 times, (m1, k2 tog) 7 times, k1.

Round 69: k2, *(m1, k2 tog) 6 times, k4. Repeat from * 8 times, (m1, k2 tog) 6 times, k2.

Round 71: k3, *(m1, k2 tog) 5 times, k6. Repeat from * 8 times, (m1, k2 tog) 5 times, k3.

Round 73: k4, *(m1, k2 tog) 4 times, k8. Repeat from * 8 times, (m1, k2 tog) 4 times, k4.

Round 75: k5, *(m1, k2 tog) 3 times, k10. Repeat from * 8 times, (m1, k2 tog) 3 times, k5.

Round 77: k6, *(m1, k2 tog) twice, k12. Repeat from * 8 times, (m1, k2 tog) twice, k6.

Round 79: k7, *m1, k2 tog, k14. Repeat from * 8 times, m1, k2 tog, k7.

Round 81: k6, *(m1, k2 tog) twice, k12. Repeat from * 8 times, (m1, k2 tog) twice, k6.

Round 83: k6, *(m1, k2 tog) 3 times, k10. Repeat from * 8 times, (m1, k2 tog) 3 times, k5.

Round 85: k4, *(m1, k2 tog) 4 times, k8. Repeat from * 8 times, (m1, k2 tog) 4 times, k4.

Round 87: k3, *(m1, k2 tog) 5 times, k6. Repeat from * 8 times, (m1, k2 tog) 5 times, k3.

Round 89: k2, *(m1, k2 tog) 6 times, k4. Repeat from * 8 times, (m1, k2 tog) 6 times, k2.

Round 91: k1, *(m1, k2 tog) 7 times, k2. Repeat from * 8 times, (m1, k2 tog) 7 times, k1.

Round 93: (m1, k2 tog) to end of round.

Repeat rounds 38–93.

Knit 4 rounds.

Repeat rounds 38–61.

Knit 8 rounds.

Next round: (m4, k2 tog) to end of round.

Next round: Knit, working k1, p1, k1, p1 in m4 of previous round.

Knit 8 rounds.

Cast off.

SHELL LACE (for bag top)

NB: Working m1 before a p2 tog, make sure the thread goes around the needle.

Cast on 13 sts.

Row 1: k2, m2, k2 tog, k7, m1, p2 tog.

Row 2: m1, p2 tog, k9, p1, k2.

Row 3: k12, m1, p2 tog.

Row 4: m1, p2 tog, k12.

Row 5: k2, (m2, k2 tog) twice, k6, m1, p2 tog.

Row 6: m1, p2 tog, k8, (p1, k2) twice.

Row 7: k14, m1, p2 tog.

Row 8: m1, p2 tog, k14.

Row 9: k2, (m2, k2 tog) 3 times, k6, m1, p2 tog.

Row 10: m1, p2 tog, k8, (p1, k2) 3 times.

Row 11: k17, m1, p2 tog.

Row 12: m1, p2 tog, k17.

Row 13: k2, (m2, k2 tog) 4 times, k7, m1, p2 tog.

Row 14: m1, p2 tog, k9, (p1, k2) 4 times.

Row 15: k21, m1, p2 tog.

Row 16: m1, p2 tog, k to end of row.

Cast off 10 sts.

Repeat rows 1–16 until length required.

Cast off.

Join seam. Press the work lightly. Stitch lace around top of bag. Line reticule with contrasting colour to match ribbon or cord threaded through holes. Add bow if desired.

36 SYRINGA

A smocked basket lining edged with exquisite lace by Joan Eckersley.

Materials
1 x 20 g ball DMC 100 cotton
Needles 1 mm (20)
Books on smocking and basket lining are available from bookshops or craft suppliers.

Cast on 13 sts.
Knit one row.
Row 1: sl 1, (k2, m1, k2 tog) twice, k4.

Row 2: k2, m2, (k2, m1, k2 tog) twice, k3.
Row 3: sl 1, k2, m1, k2 tog, k4, m1, k2 tog, k1, p1, k2.
Row 4: k6, m1, k2 tog, k2, m1, k2 tog, k3.
Row 5: sl 1, k4, m1, k2 tog, k2, m1, k2 tog, k4.
Row 6: k8, m1, k2 tog, k2, m1, k2 tog, k1.
Row 7: sl 1, (k2, m1, k2 tog) twice, k6.
Row 8: Cast off 2 sts, k12.

Repeat rows 1–8 until length required.

37 ROSETTE

The rosettes incorporate a lavender circle in the design, providing protection to curtains from insect attack.
The lavender sachet is easily removed for replenishing. Rosettes are decorative hanging from bedposts or
church pews. Use them as an interesting alternative to large fabric bows. Designed and knitted by author.

Materials

3 x 50 g balls DMC 4-ply Hermina
Needles 2 mm (14)

Measurements

Diameter of rosette 23 cm (9")
Diameter of fluted centre 12.5 cm (5")
Top rosette to tip of tie 52 cm (20½")

Back of rosette

Cast on 24 sts.
Row 1: sl 1, k20, m1, k2 tog, k1.
Row 2: m1, k2 tog, k7, p10, turn.
Row 3: sl 1, k14, m1, k2 tog, m1, k2.
Row 4: m1, k2 tog, k8, p10, turn.
Row 5: sl 1, k13, (m1, k2 tog) twice, m1, k2.
Row 6: m1, k2 tog, k9, p10, m1, k2 tog, k3.
Row 7: sl 1, k4, p10, k3, (m1, k2 tog) 3 times, m1, k2.
Row 8: m1, k2 tog, k20, turn.
Row 9: sl 1, p9, k2, (m1, k2 tog) 4 times, m1, k2.
Row 10: m1, k2 tog, k21, turn.
Row 11: sl 1, p9, k1, (m1, k2 tog) 5 times, m1, k2.
Row 12: m1, k2 tog, k12, p10, m1, k2 tog, k3.
Row 13: sl 1, k15, k2 tog, (m1, k2 tog) 5 times, k1.
Row 14: m1, k2 tog, k11, p10, turn.
Row 15: sl 1, k11, k2 tog, (m1, k2 tog) 4 times, k1.
Row 16: m1, k2 tog, k10, p10, turn.
Row 17: sl 1, k12, k2 tog, (m1, k2 tog) 3 times, k1.
Row 18: m1, k2 tog, k19, m1, k2 tog, k3.
Row 19: sl 1, k4, p10, k4, k2 tog, (m1, k2 tog) twice, k1.
Row 20: m1, k2 tog, k18, turn.
Row 21: sl 1, p9, k5, k2 tog, m1, k2 tog, k1.
Row 22: m1, k2 tog, k17, turn.
Row 23: sl 1, p9, k9.
Row 24: m1, k2 tog, k17, m1, k2 tog, k3.
Repeat rows 1–24 until back of rosette forms circle.

Centre

Cast on 9 sts, 3 sts on each of 3 needles. Work with 4th needle.
Rows 1 and 2: Knit.
Row 3: *m1, k1, repeat from * 8 times.
Row 4 and alternate rows: Knit.
Row 5: *m1, k2, repeat from * 8 times.
Row 7: *m1, k3, repeat from * 8 times.
Row 9: *m1, k4, repeat from * 8 times.
Row 11: *m1, k5, repeat from * 8 times.
Row 13: *m1, k6, repeat from * 8 times.
Row 15: *m1, k1, m1, sl 1, k1, psso, k4, repeat from * 8 times.

Row 17: *m1, k3, m1, sl 1, k1, psso, k3, repeat from * 8 times.
Row 19: *m1, k2, m1, sl 1, k1, psso, k1, m1, sl 1, k1, psso, k2. Repeat from * 8 times.
Row 21: *m1, k2, m1, sl 1, k1, psso, (m1, sl 1, k1, psso, k1) twice. Repeat from * 8 times.
Row 23: *m1, k2, (m1, sl 1, k1, psso) 3 times, k1, m1, sl 1, k1, psso. Repeat from * 8 times.
Row 25: *m1, k2, (m1, sl 1, k1, psso) 5 times. Repeat from * 8 times.
Row 26: Knit (117 sts).
Cast off loosely. Work forms an attractive fluted centre.

Inner centre

Cast on 10 sts.
Row 1: k1, (m1, k1) to end of row.
Repeat row 1 twice. Cast off.
Shape into flower centre.

Ties (make 2)

Cast on 31 sts.
Row 1: Knit.
Row 2: m1, k15, k2 tog, k14.
Row 3: As row 2.
Continue inc this way until 32 rows have been worked.
Row 33: m1, k7, k2 tog, (k6, k2 tog) twice, k6.
Row 34: m1, k14, k2 tog, k13.
Work 20 rows as row 34.
Row 55: m1, (k6, k2 tog) 3 times, k5.
Row 56: m1, k13, k2 tog, k12.
Work 14 rows as row 56.
Row 71: m1, k6, k2 tog, (k5, k2 tog) twice, k5.
Row 72: m1, k12, k2 tog, k11.
Work 14 rows as row 72.
Row 87: m1, (k5, k2 tog) 3 times, k4.
Row 88: m1, k11, k2 tog, k10.
Work 10 rows as row 88.
Row 99: m1, k5, (k2 tog, k4) 3 times.
Row 100: m1, k10, k2 tog, k9.
Work 10 rows as row 100.
Row 111: m1, (k4, k2 tog) 3 times, k3.
Row 112: m1, k9, k2 tog, k8.
Work 6 rows as row 112.
Row 119: m1, k4, (k2 tog, k3) 3 times.
Row 120: m1, k8, k2 tog, k7.
Work 6 rows as row 120.
Row 127: m1, (k3, k2 tog) 3 times, k2.
Row 128: m1, k7, k2 tog, k6.
Work 4 rows as row 128.
Row 133: m1, k3, (k2 tog, k2) 3 times.

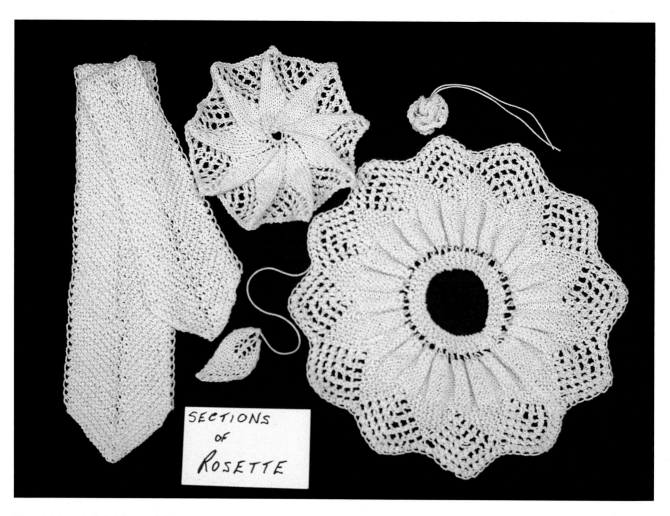

SECTIONS
OF
ROSETTE

Row 134: m1, k6, k2 tog, k5.
Work 2 rows as row 134.
Row 137: m1, (k2, k2 tog) 3 times, k1.
Row 138: m1, k5, k2 tog, k4.
Work 2 rows as row 138.
Row 141: m1, k2, (k2 tog, k1) 3 times.
Row 142: m1, k4, k2 tog, k3.
Work 1 row as row 142.
Cast off
This completes one tie of the rosette.
For a shorter version commence the work at row 55, casting on 29 sts.

Leaves

Cast on 3 sts.
Row 1: Knit.
Rows 2 and 3: K, inc 1 st at end of row.
Row 4: k2, p1, k2.
Row 5: k2, m1, k1, m1, k2.
Row 6: k2, p3, k2.
Row 7: k3, m1, k1, m1, k3.
Row 8: k2, p5, k2.

Repeat last 2 rows.
Inc until there are 17 sts on needle, always with k2 at each end of the rows.
Work 2 rows without increasing.
Next row: With front of leaf facing, k until the st before centre, sl 1, k2 tog, psso, k to end of row.
Next row: Purl (keeping garter st edge).
Repeat last 2 rows until 5 sts remain.
Next row: k2, p1, k2.
Next row: k2, k2 tog, k1.
Next row: Purl.
Next row: (k2 tog) twice.
Fasten off.
Press leaves lightly. Use as desired to trim ties.

Assembling the rosette
Make a circular sachet approximately 20 cm (8") in diameter. Insert a thin circle of wadding, add generous amount of lavender. Close the seam. Place knitted rosette and fluted circle on the lavender circle and attach. Put centre flower into position, stitch into place. Add leaves to the ties as illustrated. Sew the ties to the back of the lavender circle. Make a ribbon or cord loop to hang the rosette. Use with or without ties as preferred.

38 THE ECKERSLEY COLLECTION

Three linen handkerchiefs with lace knitted by Joan Eckersley. A perfect gift for a bride.

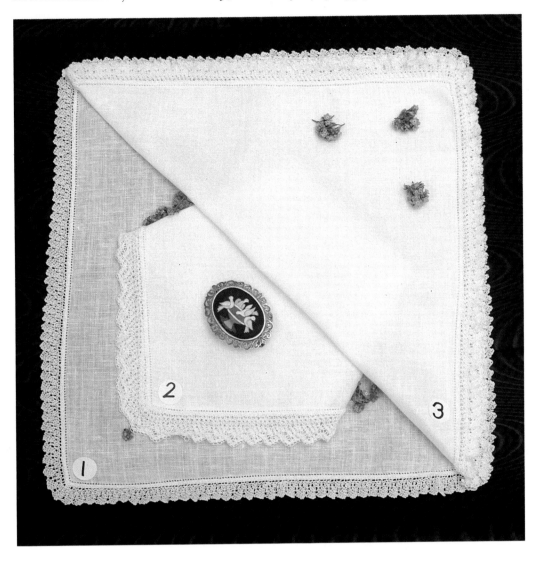

Materials
2 x 20 g balls of DMC 100 is sufficient for three handkerchiefs
Needles 1 mm (20)
Extremely fine knitting

HANDKERCHIEF 1

Cast on 11 sts.
Knit 2 rows.
Row 1: sl 1, k1, m1, k9 (12 sts).
Row 2: Knit.
Row 3: sl 1, k1, m1, k2, (m1, k2 tog) twice, k4 (13 sts).
Row 4: Knit.
Row 5: sl 1, k1, m1, k2, (m1, k2 tog) 3 times, k3 (14 sts).
Row 6: Cast off 3 sts, k10 (11 sts).
Row 7: sl 1, k10.
Row 8: Knit.
Repeat rows 1–8 until length desired.

HANDKERCHIEF 2

Cast on 7 sts.

Knit one row.

Row 1: sl 1, k2, m1, k2 tog, k1, (m1, k1) 4 times in last st, then knit the st (15 sts).

Row 2: Picot: cast on 2 sts on LH needle, k2 sts. Draw 1st st over 2nd st, k1, again. Draw thread over 1st st, k14 (15 sts).

Row 3: sl 1, k1, m1, k2 tog, k11 (15 sts).

Row 4: As row 2 (15 sts).

Row 5: sl 1, k2, m1, k2 tog, k10 (15 sts).

Row 6: As row 2 (15 sts).

Row 7: sl 1, k1, m1, k2 tog, k2, draw 8 sts over next st, k1 (7 sts).

Row 8: Knit (7 sts).

Repeat rows 1–8 until length desired.

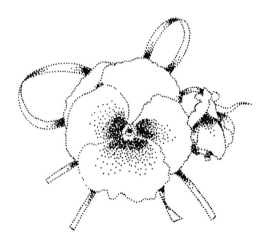

HANDKERCHIEF 3

Cast on 12 sts.

Knit one row.

Row 1: sl 1, k1, k2 tog, m1, (k1, m1, k2 tog) twice, k2 (12 sts).

Row 2: m1, k12 (13 sts).

Row 3: sl 1, k1, m1, k2 tog, k2, m1, k2 tog, k1, m1, k2 tog, k2 (13 sts).

Row 4: m1, k13 (14 sts).

Row 5: sl 1, k1, k2 tog, m1, k1, (m1, k2 tog) twice, k1, m1, k2 tog, k2 (14 sts).

Row 6: m1, k14 (15 sts).

Row 7: sl 1, k1, m1, k2 tog, k2, (m1, k2 tog) twice, k1, m1, k2 tog, k2 (15 sts).

Row 8: m1, k1, k2 tog, k12 (15 sts).

Row 9: sl 1, k1, k2 tog, m1, k1, (m1, k2 tog) twice, k1, m1, (k2 tog) twice, k1 (14 sts).

Row 10: m1, k1, k2 tog, k11 (14 sts).

Row 11: sl 1, k1, m1, k2 tog, k2, m1, k2 tog, k1, m1, (k2 tog) twice, k1 (13 sts).

Row 12: m1, k1, k2 tog, k10 (13 sts).

Row 13: sl 1, k1, k2 tog, m1, (k1, m1, k2 tog) twice, m1, k2 tog, k1 (13 sts).

Row 14: m1, k1, k2 tog, k10 (13 sts).

Row 15: sl 1, k1, m1, k2 tog, k2, m1, k2 tog, m1, (k2 tog) twice, k1.

Row 16: k12.

Repeat rows 1–16 until length desired.

39 WILLOW BASKET LID

Basket lids are an attractive way to cover a work or picnic basket. The pattern could also be used as a table centre. Edna Lomas knitted Willow.

Materials
2 x 50 g balls DMC Hermina
Set of 5 double pointed needles and circular needle; all needles 2.75 mm (12)

The looped edge made by the knit cast-off provides the holes to tie the lid to the basket handle. Use matching ribbons or knitted cords.

    The finished basket cover is 61 cm (24") in diameter.

Cast on 8 sts, divided evenly on 4 needles, knit with 5th needle.

Round 1: Knit.
Round 2: *m1, k1. Repeat from * to end of round (16 sts).
Round 3 and alternate rounds until round 49: Knit.
Round 4: *m1, k2, repeat from * to end of round (24 sts).
Round 6: *m1, k3, repeat from * to end of round (32 sts).
Round 8: *m1, k4, repeat from * to end of round (40 sts).
Round 10: *m1, k5, repeat from * to end of round (48 sts).
Round 12: *m1, k6, repeat from * to end of round (56 sts).
Round 14: *m1, k7, repeat from * to end of round (64 sts).
Round 16: *m1, k1, m1, sl 1, k1, psso, k5, repeat from * to end of round (72 sts).
Round 18: *m1, k3, m1, sl 1, k1, psso, k4, repeat from * to end of round (80 sts).
Round 20: *m1, k2, m1, sl 1, k1, psso, k1, m1, sl 1, k1, psso, k3. Repeat from * to end of round (88 sts).
Round 22: *m1, k2, (m1, sl 1, k1, psso) twice, k1, m1, sl 1, k1, psso, k2. Repeat from * to end of round (96 sts).
Round 24: *m1, k4, m1, sl 1, k1, psso, k3, m1, sl 1, k1, psso, k1. Repeat from * to end of round (104 sts).
Round 26: *m1, k11, m1, sl 1, k1, psso, repeat from * to end of round (112 sts).
Round 28: Place last 2 sts of each needle on LH needle, *m1, k1, m1, sl 1, k1, psso, (k3, m1, sl 1, k1, psso) twice, k1. Repeat from * to end of round (120 sts).
Round 30: *m1, k1, (m1, sl 1, k1, psso) twice, k1, (m1, sl 1m k1, psso) twice, k1, (m1, sl 1, k1, psso) twice. Repeat from * to end of round (128 sts).
Round 32: *m1. k1, (m1, sl 1, k1, psso) 3 times, k1, m1, sl 1, k1, psso, k3, m1, sl 1, k1, psso, k1. Repeat from * to end of round (136 sts).
Round 34: *m1, k1, (m1, sl 1, k1, psso) 4 times, k3, m1, sl 1, k1, psso, k3. Repeat from * to end of round (144 sts).
Round 36: *m1, k1, (m1, sl 1, k1, psso) 5 times, k1, (m1, sl 1, k1, psso) twice, k2. Repeat from * to end of round (152 sts).
Round 38: Change to circular needle. *m1, k1, (m1, sl 1, k1, psso) 6 times, k1, m1, sl 1, k1, psso, k3. Repeat from * to end of round (160 sts).
Round 40: *m1. k1, (m1, sl 1, k1, psso) 7 times, k5. Repeat from * to end of round (168 sts).

Round 42: *m1, k1, (m1, sl 1, k1, psso) 8 times, k4. Repeat from * to end of round (176 sts).
Round 44: *m1, k1, (m1, sl 1, k1, psso) 9 times, k3. Repeat from * to end of round (184 sts).
Round 46: *m1, k1, (m1, sl 1, k1, psso) 10 times, k2. Repeat from * to end of round (192 sts).
Round 48: *m1, k1, (m1, sl 1, k1, psso) 11 times, k1. Repeat from * to end of round (200 sts).
Round 50: *m1, k1, (m1, sl 1, k1, psso) 12 times. Repeat from * to end of round (208 sts).
Rounds 51, 52 and 53: Knit.
Round 54: *(p2 tog) twice, (m1, k1) 4 times, m1, (p2 tog) twice, p1. Repeat from * to end of round (224 sts).
Rounds 55, 56 and 57: Knit.
Round 58: Cut cotton. Place first 6 sts on RH needle. Rejoin cotton, *(k1, m1) 3 times, (p2 tog) twice, p1, (p2 tog) twice, (m1, k1) twice, m1. Repeat from * to end of round (256 sts).
Rounds 59, 60 and 61: Knit.
Round 62: *(k1, m1) 3 times, (p2 tog) twice, p3 tog, (p2 tog) twice, (m1, k1) twice, m1. Repeat from * to end of round (256 sts).
Round 63, 64 and 65: Knit.
Round 66: As round 62 (256 sts).
Rounds 67, 68 and 69: Knit.
Round 70: *(k1, m1) 4 times, (p2 tog) twice, p1, (p2 tog) twice, m1, (k1, m1) 3 times. Repeat from * to end of round (320 sts).
Rounds 71, 72 and 73: Knit.
Round 74: *(k1, m1) 4 times, (p2 tog) 3 times, p1, (p2 tog) 3 times, m1, (k1, m1) 3 times. Repeat from * to end of round (352 sts).
Rounds 75, 76 and 77: Knit.
Round 78: *(k1, m1) 4 times, (p2 tog) 3 times, p3 tog, (p2 tog) 3 times, m1, (k1, m1) 3 times. Repeat from * to end of round (352 sts).
Rounds 79, 80 and 81: Knit.
Round 82: *(k1, m1) 5 times, (p2 tog) 3 times, p1, (p2 tog) 3 times, (m1, k1) 4 times, m1. Repeat from * to end of round (416 sts).
Rounds 83, 84 and 85: Knit.
Round 86: *(k1, m1) 5 times, (p2 tog) 4 times, p1, (p2 tog) 4 times, (m1, k1) 4 times, m1. Repeat from * to end of round (448 sts).
Rounds 87, 88 and 89: Knit.
Round 90: *(k1, m1) 5 times, (p2 tog) 4 times, p3 tog, (p2 tog) 4 times, (m1, k1) 4 times, m1. Repeat from * to end of round (448 sts).
Rounds 91, 92 and 93: Knit.
Round 94: As round 90 (448 sts).
Rounds 95, 96 and 97: Knit.
Round 98: *(k1, m1) 6 times, (p2 tog) 4 times, p1, (p2 tog) 4 times, (m1, k1) 5 times, m1. Repeat from * to end of round (512 sts).
Rounds 99, 100 and 101: Knit.

Round 102: *(k1, m1) 6 times, (p2 tog) 5 times, p1, (p2 tog) 5 times, (m1, k1) 5 times, m1. Repeat from * to end of round (544 sts).

Rounds 103, 104 and 105: Knit.

Round 106: *(k1, m1) 7 times, (p2 tog) 5 times, p1, (p2 tog) 5 times, (m1, k1) 6 times, m1. Repeat from * to end of round (608 sts).

Round 107: *k1 into st under st on RH needle, k37. Repeat from * to end of round (624 sts).

Rounds 108 and 109: Knit.

Cast off knitwise thus:
K1, *k2 tog, m1, k2 tog. Turn, p1, *[(k1, p1) twice, k1] in next st, p1, sl 1 purlwise. Turn. Cast off 7 sts (one st left on RH needle)* Repeat from *–* to last 5 sts, k3 tog, m1, k2 tog. Turn, p1, (k1, p1) twice, k1 in next st, p1, sl 1 purlwise. Turn.
Cast off remaining sts.
For a larger loop on your edging make 9 sts instead of the 5 sts given above.

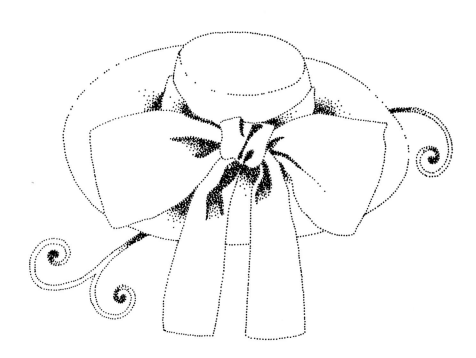

40 VANDYKE TASSEL

A tassel with many uses. Suitable for curtain tie-backs, key tassels, blind pulls or wall hangings. Make them in fine thread to trim a dainty cushion. Tassels made by author.

Materials
Small quantity of 4-ply cotton
Set of 4 double pointed needles 2 mm (14)

Cast on 45 sts, 15 sts on each of 3 needles. Work with 4th needle.
Purl 3 rounds.
Round 4: (k2 tog, k5, m1, k1, m1, k5, k2 tog) to end of round.

Round 5: Knit.
Repeat rounds 4 and 5, 14 times.
Round 34: (k1, k2 tog) to end of round.
Purl 3 rounds.
Round 38: Knit.
Round 39: (k1, p1) to end of round.
Work 11 rounds as Round 39.
Cast off.

Make an ordinary tassel by winding yarn around a piece of card. Slip this tassel inside the knitted one. Draw together the open top of the knitted tassel. When fastening it off, run the needle through the top of the inside tassel and the knitted one, securing both. Then thread a piece of yarn through the lower part of the tassel head (at round 38). Draw up the thread, and secure. Trim the visible threads of the inner tassel.
Knit a length of fine cord and attach to tassel head. A weight can be inserted inside the tassel, making it an ideal trim for a garden or picnic cloth, eliminating the irritation of a wind-swept table cloth. The tassel can also be used as a blind trim, simply attached to the blind cord.

Cord

Cast on 3 sts.
k3, do not turn. Slide sts to other end of needle. Pull yarn firmly. Repeat from *–* to required length.

Two-tone tassel

A two-coloured tassel is knitted thus:
Cast on in contrast (second) colour.
Purl 3 rounds.
Change to main colour.
Change to contrast colour on round 34.
Change to main colour on round 38.
Make the inner tassel in contrast colour.
This tassel is useful for toning in with your decor.

BIBLIOGRAPHY

Abbey, Barbara: *Knitting Lace*, Schoolhouse Press, Pittsville, Wisconsin, reprinted 1993

De Dillmont, Thérèse: *Encyclopedia of Needlework*, DMC Publication, Mulhouse, France 1924

Fancy and Practical Knitting, 1897, The Butterick Publishing Co., London and New York

Klickman, Flora: *The Modern Knitting Book*, published by *The Girls' Own and Woman's Magazine*, London 1914

Lewis, Susanna E: *Knitting Lace*, Taunton Press, USA 1992

Mrs Leach's Fancy Work Basket, R. S. Cartwright, London 1887

Needlecraft Practical Journals, W. Briggs & Co. Ltd, 34 Cannon Street, Manchester, c.1911, 1930

Roediger, Fiona: *Smocking Ideas*, Kangaroo Press, Sydney 1993
—*Heirloom Smocking*, Kangaroo Press, Sydney 1995

Rutt, Richard, The Rt Rev.: *A History of Hand Knitting*, B.T. Batsford Ltd, London 1987

Sibbald and Souter: *Dainty Work for Busy Fingers*, S.W. Partridge & Co. Ltd, London 1915

Thomas, Mary: *Mary Thomas's Book of Knitting Patterns*, Hodder & Stoughton Ltd, London 1985

Weldon's Practical Knitter, series published by Weldon Ltd, The Strand, London c.1890–1911

Wright, Mary: *Cornish Guernseys and Knit Frocks*, Alison Hodges, Cornwall 1979
—*Granny's Lace Knitting and Great Granny's Lace Knitting*, self published, Cornwall 1986

Zimmerman, Elizabeth: *Knitter's Almanac*, Dover, New York 1981
—*Knitting Around*, Schoolhouse Press, Pittsville, Wisconsin 1989

GUILDS

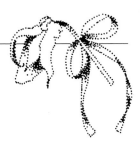

The British Knitting and Crochet Guild
Membership Secretary
228 Chester Road
North Kidderminster
Worcestershire DY10 1TH
United Kingdom

Handknitters Guild Inc.
Meat Market Craft Centre
North Melbourne Victoria 3051

Knitters Guild NSW Inc.
The Secretary
25 Langer Avenue
Caringbah NSW 2229

SUPPLIERS

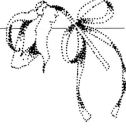

DMC Needlecraft Pty Ltd
51-55 Carrington Road
Marrickville NSW 2204
(02) 9559 3088

Fyshwick Antique Centre
72 Kembla Street
Fyshwick ACT 2609
(06) 280 4541

Queanbeyan Books and Prints
Millhouse Gallery
49 Collett Street
Queanbeyan NSW 2620
(06) 297 3067

Kia Lloyds
61 McNicholl Street
Hughes ACT 2605
(06) 281 5301
Qualified knitting instructor; yarns and advice.
Mail order. SAE please.

Mill Hill Books
(Graham and Dallas Nott)
PO Box 80
Maleny Qld 4552
(07) 494 2081

INDEX